CFA Institute

BRIDGING THE GAP: ENSURING EFFECTIVE NON-GAAP AND PERFORMANCE REPORTING

CFA Institute is the global association of investment professionals that sets the standards for professional excellence. We are a champion for ethical behavior in investment markets and a respected source of knowledge in the global financial community.

Our mission is to lead the investment profession globally by promoting the highest standards of ethics, education, and professional excellence for the ultimate benefit of society.

ISBN: 978-1-942713-31-9
November 2016

Contents

Executive Summary

This paper is the second of a two-part publication on non-GAAP financial measures (NGFMs), interchangeably referred to as alternative performance measures (APMs).[1] In Section 1.3, NGFMs or APMs are defined as financial measures derived from adjusting GAAP/IFRS measures. The definition does not include other key performance indicators (KPIs) and/or operational measures (e.g., customer retention rate, sales per square foot).

This paper builds on Part 1 of the publication, which articulated investors' uses, expectations, and concerns regarding NGFMs. The current paper proposes ways of strengthening the overall performance reporting framework of which any NGFMs ought to remain only as supplemental and informative measures—and not to undermine or supplant GAAP/IFRS measures of performance, liquidity, and financial position.

[1]The distinction between GAAP and non-GAAP line items is relatively clear in the United States because of the fairly detailed income statement presentation requirements. The boundaries are less clear under IFRS, however, because there are fewer specified income statement line items and there is a requirement to provide additional line items and subtotals if they are necessary for understanding an entity's performance.

Increasing Regulatory Scrutiny

Several NGFM shortcomings have caught the attention of various leading securities regulatory organizations, which have cautioned about, issued guidelines for, and continue to monitor reporting of NGFMs. The US SEC has issued guidelines at different junctures, starting with Regulation G (Reg G) requirements. Reg G, effective in 2003, was issued in the aftermath of the late 1990s—the era of the internet dot-com bubble, during which several egregious incidences of NGFM misreporting occurred. The SEC updated its guidance in 2010 and, most recently, in May 2016 through Compliance and Disclosure Interpretation (C&DI) documents. NGFMs also accounted for 14% (the fourth-highest percentage) of SEC comment letters written to companies on questionable reporting practices for the year 2015 (Deloitte 2015).[2]

[2]Only management discussion & analysis (MD&A) sections, revenue, and fair value measurements had higher frequencies of SEC comment letters issued to companies.

Prior to the SEC's issuance of the May 2016 C&DI, its senior personnel had made speeches signaling the commission's intention to intensify scrutiny over reporting of NGFMs.[3] The SEC has since issued 30 NGFM-related comment letters to companies, and there is evidence of immediate improvement in NGFM reporting by US companies (Kaplan, Samit, Isaacson, and Becker 2016).[4]

Parallel efforts to curtail misleading reporting of these measures have been undertaken by other major securities regulatory organizations, including, the European Securities Markets Authority (ESMA) and the International Organization of Securities Commission (IOSCO). These two organizations have respectively updated their guidance in 2016.[5] Other countries' securities regulators have similarly provided guidelines at different junctures (e.g., Australia, Canada, and the United Kingdom).

These guidelines from different securities regulators are quite similar in their key areas of focus. All aim to enhance the transparency, comparability, and consistency of NGFM reporting, as well as to ensure it has no undue prominence. These actions aim to reduce the risk of investors being misled by NGFM reporting.

The heightened scrutiny, clarifications, and strengthened guidelines by the aforementioned securities regulators may have contributed to curbing misleading and low-quality reporting of NGFMs (e.g., egregious exclusion of recurring cash expenses by some companies in their NGFM calculations). Indeed, academic evidence shows that after the 2003 Reg G requirements, many US companies that were hitherto reporting low-quality NGFMs stopped reporting these measures. A question remains in the eyes of different market participants, however, of whether these existing guidelines and other regulatory monitoring and sanctioning measures go far enough in accomplishing their intended objectives. These questions arise with a backdrop of seemingly never-ending NGFM misreporting episodes highlighted by the media and other market commentators.

[3]Chairperson Mary Jo White, Chief Accountant Jim Schnurr, Interim Chief Accountant Wesley Becker, and Director of Corporate Finance Keith Higgins have all made speeches cautioning against misleading reporting of NGFMs.

[4]The authors analyzed 100 companies and found that 79 of these companies altered the presentation of NGFMs in their earnings releases in conformance with SEC updated guidance.

[5]IOSCO had issued a cautionary statement in 2002, a consultative document in 2014, and updated guidelines in June 2016. ESMA's predecessor body, the Committee of European Securities Regulators (CESR), had similarly issued guidelines on APMs.

Our Involvement and Approach

As noted in Part 1 of this publication, our commentary has been prompted by a call from some of our members for the articulation of a CFA Institute position on NGFMs. The premise is that investor demand and companies' desire to communicate NGFMs will likely persist for the foreseeable future, and hence curtailing incidences of misleading NGFM reporting is necessary. Reporting companies' management, those charged with governance, securities regulators, accounting standard setters, and auditors could all benefit from considering the investor perspectives articulated here.

This paper largely reflects CFA Institute member perspectives, obtained through a global survey on the uses, concerns, and expectations around the reporting of these measures.[6] Our survey had 558 respondents (3.5% response rate) with the following attributes, as shown in the Appendix: mostly buy-side players (analysts and portfolio managers, 65.7%); predominantly focused on equity (73.8%); mostly long term in investment horizon (57.2%); and fairly spread out in their coverage across sectors.

Headline Findings

Member survey results provide a high-level assessment of the perceived adequacy of guidelines, monitoring, and enforcement actions. These results and accompanying comments reveal that many investors expect more outcomes from securities regulatory actions (i.e., whenever these bodies undertake to improve NGFM reporting). There is a general sense that the "bite" from securities regulators (e.g., enforcement actions) needs to match their "bark" (i.e., overall intent to curb misleading NGFM reporting). That said, the survey results and a few respondent comments also suggest that there are at least some investors, albeit a seeming minority, who believe regulators should not interfere with NGFM reporting in any form. In other words, there is a diversity of expectations on the role, if any, that regulators should have in imposing discipline around the reporting of NGFMs.

In this publication, we take the view that securities regulators have a vital role in imposing discipline around the reporting of NGFMs. However, we consider current and potentially strengthened regulatory actions (i.e., guidelines, monitoring, and enforcement actions) to be only necessary but not sufficient as far as ensuring that companies communicate only the highest-quality measures of performance, liquidity, and financial condition. We believe

[6]Our member survey questionnaire had 19 questions, some more detailed than others. Response levels to each question varied from about 400 to 558 responses.

other key actors involved in supplying financial information for capital markets participants also have a vital role to play in ensuring only high-quality NGFM reporting occurs.

For instance, NGFM concerns should serve as a catalyst for the International Accounting Standards Board (IASB) and the US Financial Accounting Standards Board (FASB) to enhance their primary financial statements' presentation and classification requirements, including defining key subtotals. Our survey results show that most investors expect and support the idea of standard setters providing guidance around NGFMs presented within financial statements. Another of our key findings is that there is strong support for some level of assurance on NGFMs.

In our recommendations, we articulate additional steps required by regulators, auditors, audit committees, and investors to ensure the effective reporting of these measures and the strengthening of NGFMs' overall quality (i.e., informative and reliable NGFMs).

1. Overview

1.1. Factors Influencing NGFM Supply and Demand

Figure 1.1 outlines the broad factors shaping the supply of and demand for NGFMs. We elaborate on these factors through this report.

Figure 1.1. Factors Influencing NGFM Quantity and Quality

1.1.1. Investor Demand

Part 1 of this publication showed that NGFMs are widely used by investors, and it also highlighted the factors influencing investor demand for NGFMs. These factors include investors applying NGFMs as inputs for assessing companies' performance, valuation, and overall accounting quality.

1.1.2. Supply Side: Companies' Management Reporting Incentives

Companies reporting NGFMs do so from two broad motives: (a) to better inform investors on entity-specific performance, liquidity, and financial position; (b) to opportunistically manage investors' perceptions of companies' performance and financial health. Both academic research (Bhattacharya, Black, Christensen, and Larson 2003) and investor feedback (Part 1 of this publication) reveal the valuation relevance and information content of NGFMs. Academic evidence also shows that managers apply NGFMs in an opportunistic manner to meet earnings targets and to portray a more positive performance picture than that conveyed by the reported GAAP measures (Black and Christensen 2009; Isidiro and Marques 2009).

Furthermore, the corporate governance mechanisms within companies, such as board independence and effectiveness of audit committees, can affect NGFM quality (Frankel, McVay, and Soliman 2011).

1.1.3. Accounting Standards Lagging Evolving Business Model Needs

Several observers have asserted that NGFMs are symptomatic of the absence of a robust performance reporting framework within existing accounting standards. In addition, many stakeholders hold the view that recognition and measurement requirements have not always fully caught up with the needs of evolving business models, complex transactions, and contractual arrangements. NGFMs and other key performance metrics provide supplemental information, filling the gaps within GAAP/IFRS. We discuss these issues in Section 2.

1.1.4. Regulators' Imposed Restraints

Securities regulators' guidelines, monitoring, and enforcement actions have the potential to curtail low-quality NGFMs. Hence, the extent to which companies still report misleading NGFMs could in part reflect the extent to which securities regulatory measures have been ineffective. We discuss these issues in Section 4.

1.2. Summary of Recommendations

NGFMs will likely be both needed by investors and communicated by companies for the foreseeable future. To start, as discussed in Section 2, existing financial statements are general purpose in nature and are not designed to meet any particular user's full information needs, which naturally creates a need for supplemental information. In addition, perceived shortcomings within existing financial statement presentation requirements, such as lack of definition of particular subtotals, could be seen as a factor in NGFMs' proliferation.

Nonetheless, as Young (2013) hypothesizes, NGFMs or APMs are likely to be inevitable even if accounting standard setters could craft a robust and enhanced performance reporting framework. Young draws analogies between the need for NGFMs and the prevalence of supplemental measures in other disciplines (e.g., GDP forecasting and school league tables), observing that there is usually an incentive to control the message or highlight information signals that the standardized reporting framework may be constraining. Hence, it is likely an insuperable goal to have a one-size-fits-all performance reporting framework that reflects the specificities of every conceivable business model and accommodates every view of how to best represent performance. The key performance reporting policy considerations then ought to be (a) how to enhance the performance reporting requirements to minimize the need for alternative measures and (b) how to put discipline around the reporting of NGFMs so that they do not mislead capital market participants.

Correspondingly, our recommendations advocate for the following: (a) potentially preemptive measures, such as the role of accounting standard setters in enhancing the performance, liquidity, and financial condition presentation requirements within accounting standards; and (b) measures to enhance the quality of NGFMs (i.e., economic relevance, comparability, transparency, consistency, and reliability).

Figure 1.2 portrays the different actors who have a role in ensuring the effective communication of NGFMs.

Figure 1.2. Summary of Recommendations to Enhance NGFM Quality

1.2.1. Responsibilities for Reducing the Need for Certain NGFMs

Accounting Standard Setters

The expected role of accounting standard setters with respect to NGFMs is twofold:

- The first role is a preemptive one, as alluded to in public statements by IASB chair Hans Hoogervorst and FASB members Marc Siegel and Tom Linsmeier.[7] These board members acknowledge the relationship between an enhanced presentation of primary financial statements (e.g., defining subtotals) and a reduced need for NGFMs.

[7]Linsmeier's term at the FASB expired in 2016. See Linsmeier (2016), Siegel (2016), and Hoogervorst (2015).

By implication, the linkage between accounting standards' financial statements presentation requirements and NGFMs creates a need for the IASB and the FASB to focus on, appropriately scope, and prioritize investor requirements. In addition, they should expedite the completion of the performance reporting or primary financial statements project so as to meaningfully address any information shortfalls within the mandated accounting requirements that may be leading to the current types of NGFMs.

- The second role is for accounting standard setters to provide requirements that ensure faithful and fair representation of NGFMs if and when these are presented in financial statements (e.g., under IFRS reporting). The need for accounting standard setters to provide guidance arises because ESMA and IOSCO guidelines pertain only to NGFMs presented outside the financial statements. Indeed, our survey results show that 65% of respondents expect accounting standard setters to provide guidance related to NGFMs. The IASB has been considering this need under the Principles of Disclosure project.[8]

1.2.2. Responsibilities for Enhancing NGFM Quality (Relevance, Transparency, Comparability, and Consistency)

Securities Regulators Strengthen Guidelines, Positive Reinforcement, and Sanctions

As noted, there has been a raft of issued and updated guidelines across different jurisdictions. An "acid test" of their effectiveness will be the extent to which companies' reporting behavior improves.

Our survey results also show that investors expect more from securities regulators' guidelines and enforcement actions than is currently occurring. This finding may seem odd given that these guidelines aim to protect investors and address areas that can result in investors being misled or not fully informed by company-reported NGFMs.

We recognize that investors who have assessed current guidelines as ineffective may not be fully familiar with the fine print of each respective regulator's guidelines (SEC, IOSCO, ESMA). Investors' likely lack of detailed knowledge of the aforementioned guidelines should not be surprising because these guidelines (a) do not undergo the same level of relatively extensive consultative outreach to investors as is the case for accounting standards

[8]See the June 2015 staff paper at www.ifrs.org/Meetings/MeetingDocs/IASB/2015/June/AP11G-Disclosure%20Initiative.pdf.

and (b) are mostly articulated as high-level principles, and as such, can be subject to varied interpretation by companies.

Potential investor knowledge of particular guidelines is also hampered by different securities regulators using differing language in their guidelines to address overlapping and similar NGFM-related areas of focus (e.g., "define," "label," "explain," "reconcile," "have comparatives").

Moreover, when evaluating the effectiveness of regulator guidelines, investors tend to give more weight to observed reporting outcomes rather than to the intent of related guidelines. The seemingly unending episodes of misleading NGFM reporting covered by media outlets and investor observations of company NGFM reporting practices likely color investors' perception of regulatory guidelines' potency and effectiveness.

Despite these criticisms, we encourage regulators to continue to strengthen the guidance as appropriate, monitor and question misleading NGFM reporting, and pursue enforcement where appropriate. There is also scope for them to pursue positive reinforcement of informative and consistent NGFM reporting by creating platforms for showcasing examples of "best" or "least concerning" NGFM reporting practices.

An Expanded Role for Auditors

A 2014 PwC survey found that only 22% of its investor respondents considered NGFMs to be sufficiently reliable. Correspondingly, our member survey results show that 80.8% of survey respondents expect some form of assurance for NGFMs. Notwithstanding these expectations, there is a discernible need for further and increased outreach to investors by audit standard setters and auditors on the topic of NGFM assurance.

Existing audit standards requirements (e.g., the Public Company Accounting Oversight Board [PCAOB] and the International Auditing and Assurance Standards Board) and public disclosure of existing auditor reporting practices do not make it any easier for investors and other stakeholders to readily discern the extent and quality of related assurance, if any, provided by auditors on NGFMs. Poignantly, SEC Chair Mary Jo White in a December 2015 speech to the American Institute of Certified Public Accountants (AICPA) asked the audience of auditing professionals, "Are there appropriate controls over the calculation of non-GAAP measures?"

Increased investor outreach related to the assurance of NGFMs can accomplish the following.

- *Build awareness.* Outreach can help to build awareness for investors on the exact state of play in relation to either the level or lack of assurance provided for information reported within or outside the financial statements, including NGFMs. As observed in other audit matters, information gaps about auditors' responsibilities and applied methodology can lead to "expectation gaps" between auditors and stakeholders. Building awareness could reduce such gaps, should they exist.
- *Clarify investor expectations on appropriate levels of assurance.* In Section 5, we discuss different levels or types of assurance proposed by several market commentators (e.g., Joshi, Joseph, and Velandy 2014). We also recognize that the role of auditors and level of assurance required for NGFMs are under review by audit standards regulators, such as PCAOB. Any further development or formulation of NGFM assurance requirements should be informed by investor expectations.

Audit Committees and Boards of Directors Should Strengthen Oversight of NGFMs

Those charged with governance in reporting entities, including audit committees and boards of directors, have a critical role to play in ensuring companies are not communicating misleading NGFMs. The Center for Audit Quality (2016) issued some useful guidelines for audit committees to take an active role in ensuring the transparency, consistency, and comparability of NGFMs. Audit committees should also highlight any outcomes of oversight activities regarding NGFMs in their audit committee reports.

Academic research (Frankel, McVay, and Soliman 2011) shows that board independence is positively correlated with NGFM quality. A company's board of directors should also ensure that executive compensation is not linked to rosier-than-warranted NGFMs in a manner that incentivizes executive management to take disproportionate risks—a matter that can be of concern for investors, as discussed in the first part of this publication.

Investor and Sell-Side Analyst Activism

As discussed in the first part of this publication and other investor-oriented publications (e.g., CFA Society United Kingdom 2015; Parker 2016), many investors find NGFMs useful. Often, however, they also consider certain exclusions made in NGFM calculations to be inappropriate—especially those that are recurring expenses (e.g., stock option expenses). Consequently, sell-side analysts and buy-side investors ought to, where possible, use any platforms of access to company management to actively engage and directly convey their views on any exclusions that they find inappropriate.

Investors also need to probe and push company management for more-comprehensive explanations of why all the chosen adjustments made while calculating NGFMs are considered incrementally informative of the reporting entity's performance. In other words, if there is a growing concern about NGFM quality, investors have a duty to directly push companies for better reporting of these measures across all locations, even under a voluntary reporting premise.

We recognize that company management's rebuttal to investor queries may be that these measures are voluntary and any investor can make further analytical adjustments. Nonetheless, as we argued in Part 1 of this publication, the big-picture objective is to ensure that companies provide all market participants with the best starting point for making any further analytical adjustments when communicating about their performance, liquidity, or financial position.

Companies' Management: Ultimately Responsible for Quality

The most important and overarching role for improving the quality of NGFMs lies with companies' management. Management ought to (a) ensure NGFMs are meant only to incrementally inform, not mislead, investors; (b) ensure reliable NGFMs are communicated as a result of robust internal controls and procedures; and (c) conform to all existing and emerging regulatory guidelines around these measures. In addition, management responsibilities should include ensuring that NGFMs are reviewed by disclosure committees and the internal audit function (CAQ 2016; Aughton and Burns 2016).

We also recognize that the location of NGFMs (within or outside the financial statements) has a bearing on the scope of regulatory oversight and the level of assurance on the measures. That said, companies' management ought to provide only high-quality NGFMs across all platforms of communication and have transparent communication of these measures. We further discuss these recommendations in different sections of this publication.

1.3. Definition and Scope

1.3.1. Definition

SEC Regulation G and IOSCO guidance define a non-GAAP financial measure as *"a numerical measure of a registrant's historical or future financial performance, financial position, or cash flows that:*

- *"excludes amounts, or is subject to adjustments that have the effect of excluding amounts, that are included in the most directly comparable measure calculated and presented in accordance with GAAP…; or*
- *"includes amounts, or is subject to adjustments that have the effect of including amounts, that are excluded from the most directly comparable measure so calculated and presented."*

ESMA provides a definition similar to that from the SEC and IOSCO and refers to the following:

- Accounting framework (e.g., IFRS) instead of GAAP
- APMs instead of NGFMs

In other words, NGFMs/APMs are derived by adjusting a GAAP/IFRS line item or subtotal. **Table 1.1** has examples of NGFMs as well as examples of other KPIs.

Table 1.1. Examples of NGFM versus Other Metrics

NGFMs/APMs	Other Metrics, Key Performance Indicators
• Adjusted revenue • Adjusted net income • EBITDA • Adjusted EBITDA • EBITDAR • EBIT • Adjusted EPS • Free cash flow • Funds from operation • Net debt • Unbilled deferred revenue • Book-to-bill ratio • Orders and order backlog • Return on capital employed (adjusted)	• Same store sales • Average revenue per customer or user • Revenue per available room • Sales per square foot • Customer retention

1.3.2. Scope

This publication focuses on company NGFM reporting practices, which fall under the purview of securities regulators' oversight and are directly subject to management discretion and attendant issues. For example, issues of managed perception of performance usually arise with company-reported NGFMs. Street earnings or data aggregator NGFMs are also outside the scope of this publication.

Other KPIs, including non-financial measures, are outside the scope of this publication as well. We recognize, however, that similar to NGFMs, these other measures are an important part of the overall corporate performance reporting framework (Chapman and Vaessen 2016; Institute of Chartered Accountants of Scotland 2016; Lev and Gu 2016).

2. Existing Accounting Framework and NGFMs

This section examines how the existing accounting framework potentially contributes to the proliferation of NGFMs. Conversely, in both this section and Section 3, we explore how enhancing accounting standards could have a preventative or preemptive role with respect to the need for certain NGFMs.

The factors we consider in this section include the extent to which current financial reporting requirements reflects evolving business models; challenges with recognition and measurement requirements; and the presentation and classification of primary financial statements (income statement, balance sheet, and cash flow statement).

2.1. Evolving Business Models and Accounting Framework

During the last few decades, a significant evolution and a seismic, structural shift have taken place in the nature of business models. Emergent "business model" developments have been characterized by the following:

- Complex contractual arrangements with customers (e.g., bundled goods, services, and intellectual property licenses)
- Complex financial instruments
- Complex financing arrangements
- Evolving value chains (e.g., sharing economy business models)
- Increasing levels of intangible assets across different types of businesses

Yet, there is a frequently cited view to the effect that accounting requirements have not always fully caught up with, and do not always adequately reflect, the economics of these complex features within increasingly complex business models. As Dechow and Schrand (2004) point out, such concerns about the accounting framework being antiquated have long existed. They describe concerns about declines in earnings quality reflected in different academic studies with an empirical analysis of earnings quality trends.[9] For instance:

- Lev and Zarowin (1999) reported a decline in the value relevance of earnings and book value of equity during the 1978–96 period.[10] Lev and Gu (2016) provide extended empirical evidence showing that the decline in value relevance of key financial statement components has occurred from 1950 to 2013. The noted decline is observed not just for earnings and book value of equity but also for key income statement and balance sheet components, such as sales; cost of sales; selling, general, and administrative (SG&A) expenses; assets; and liabilities.

- Other studies (Collins, Maydew, and Weiss 1997; Francis and Schipper 1999) report a decline in earnings relevance but a net increase in the relevance of book equity and aggregate financial statements during a four-decade period (1952 to 1994). However, these findings were contradicted by subsequent studies (Brown, Lo, and Lyss 1999; Chang 1999), whose results agreed with those of Lev and Zarowin (1999)—namely, that both earnings and book value of equity have had declines in their value relevance.

- Dechow and Schrand (2004) explain the decline in earnings quality as primarily arising from continuously evolving business models. The authors observe that practitioners expressed concerns about the declining relevance of accounting information, a focal point during the accounting standards updates of the 1990s. Many commentators at the time described US GAAP as being developed and appropriate for manufacturing companies. The authors also note that the Lev and Zarowin (1999) study found that US companies that increased their R&D expenditure between 1976 and 1995 experienced a statistically significant decline in the relationship between earnings and stock returns, whereas companies with decreased R&D spending experienced an increase. Using 1950 to 2013 data, Lev and Gu (2016) affirm that the observed decline in the value relevance of financial statement components primarily relates to increasingly pervasive R&D and intangible asset–intensive companies. US private sector investment in intangible assets has been rising and now outstrips the declining investment in tangible assets.

The general question of how up to date accounting requirements are for the modern economy is a matter of ongoing commentary. For example, Sherman and Young, in a 2016

[9]Dechow and Schrand (2004) define earnings quality as the extent to which earnings annuitize intrinsic value. They also assume stock prices represent companies' intrinsic value, although they acknowledge that there are many junctures at which stock price does not effectively represent intrinsic value (e.g., bubble periods).

[10]Value relevance of information means that there is a statistically significant association between that particular information and stock returns or changes in stock price.

Harvard Business Review feature titled "Where Financial Reporting Still Falls Short," discuss a range of perceived shortcomings, including fair value accounting. Another popular criticism or perceived indicator of increasing irrelevance of financial statements is that balance sheets do not reflect intangible assets—a significant part of the modern economy (as discussed in the 2015 Federation of European Accountants discussion paper "Future of Corporate Reporting — Creating the Dynamics for Change" at www.fee.be).

Lev and Gu (2016) expound on the shortcomings of the current accounting treatment of intangible assets, including, in their view, the unjustified,[11] inconsistent accounting treatment between acquired and internally generated intangible assets. This noted inconsistent accounting treatment can result in a company with exactly the same nature and portfolio of intangible assets, reporting differing ROEs depending on whether it has adopted either an acquisition based or organic growth strategy. Some investors have also aired concerns[12] about the noted inconsistent accounting treatment of intangible assets (Papa and Peters 2016; Financial Reporting Council 2014). These mentioned concerns can negatively affect companies' reported earnings quality (Melumad and Nissim 2008).

Admittedly, there can sometimes appear to be inconsistencies across different flavors or sources of criticisms toward the existing accounting framework. Can economically relevant and complete balance sheets for complex business models and non-volatile,[13] "high-quality" earnings really be reported at the same time? Other points of commentary highlight problems in implementation (e.g., subjectivity of measurements) rather than establishing per se the current accounting standards' lack of relevance.[14]

The broader point is that any potential limitations of financial reporting requirements naturally lead to an information shortfall and a corresponding need for supplemental information to enable investors to assess the value creation potential of complex and multi-faceted

[11]Lev and Gu (2016) challenge the justification provided by accounting standard setters for not recognizing intangible assets—namely, measurement unreliability. They provide examples illustrating that measurement unreliability can also apply to acquired intangible assets.

[12]Some investors also expressed concerns about the double-counting of expenses as a result of amortizing certain acquired intangible assets (e.g., customer relationships) while concurrently incurring ongoing SG&A expenses with respect to maintaining these acquired customers.

[13]Unless, of course, intangibles are recognized at historical cost, as proposed by Lev and Gu (2016). Volatility is mainly associated with fair value recognition. But, it remains questionable whether an amortized cost recognition approach for intangible assets would yield the most useful information for investors. The amortized cost versus fair value choice is often one between being "precise and economically irrelevant" versus "being approximately accurate and economically relevant."

[14]Sherman and Young (2016) highlight that during the euro sovereign debt crisis, banks wrote down similar Greek lending exposures and bonds that had observable market data, with variations in write-downs ranging from 21% to 51%.

business models. NGFMs could be seen as just one subset of supplemental information that investors require over and above that provided by the accounting framework.

2.2. Recognition and Measurement Requirements and NGFMs

Several shortcomings of certain recognition and measurement requirements have been posited as reasons for NGFMs. These shortcomings include the following: (a) interpretation complexity for investors; (b) stakeholder disagreement with specific requirements; (c) the general-purpose nature of accounting information; and (d) the possibility that preparers may be attempting to offset the aggregate effects of a conservatism bias within accounting requirements and financial statements.

2.2.1. Investor Interpretation Complexity

Certain recognition and measurement requirements can contribute to interpretation complexity for users of financial statements. For example, pension re-measurements related to actuarial gains or losses are, in some instances, reclassified from other comprehensive income (OCI) to the income statement under US GAAP using the corridor smoothing approach.[15] Investors may struggle to decipher how this accounting approach reflects the economic reality of defined benefit plans. Former IASB Chairman David Tweedie's joke about the corridor approach, when it was an accounting option under IFRS, sums up the situation: *"You might as well take the number of miles to the moon, multiplied by the size of your granny's shoes, and then divide by the number you first thought of."*

More broadly, the use of OCI with items being reclassified to the income statement (i.e., "recycled") in some cases (e.g., available for securities re-measurements) and not in others (e.g., not required for actuarial gains or losses under the updated IFRS requirements) can be confusing for stakeholders as they wonder, "Why 'recycle' some OCI line items and not others?" Other areas of complexity for many investors include the multiple hedge accounting approaches in accounting for derivatives (Papa and Peters 2013). Overall, these areas of accounting complexity could contribute to a need for "clean" earnings measures by some investors.

[15]The corridor smoothing approach is applicable whenever the cumulative actuarial gains or losses exceed a corridor of the greater of the projected benefit obligation (PBO) or plan assets. The amount exceeding the corridor must, at a minimum, be amortized over the plan participants' remaining working lives (Shamrock 2012).

2.2.2. Limits to Usefulness of Reporting Outcomes from Accounting Standards

As discussed in the first part of this publication, stakeholder disagreement or the limited usefulness that investors derive from reporting outcomes yielded by existing accounting standards requirements can be a reason for NGFM-related adjustments.[16] For example, the following NGFM adjustments related to the following income statement line items sometimes reflect stakeholder disagreement with specific, underlying accounting standard requirements:

- Stock-based compensation expenses by many technology companies (From our member survey results, we infer that the disagreement with accounting standard requirements to treat stock-based compensation as expenses tends to be mainly a technology sector preparer viewpoint.)
- Goodwill impairment
- Business combination-related costs, including amortization of acquired intangibles

Other NGFM adjustments, such as those related to fair value, pension, and currency re-measurements, are made because of stakeholders' desire for particular information attributes (e.g., sustainable earnings) rather than necessarily resulting from a disagreement with accounting requirements.[17]

2.2.3. General Purpose Accounting Standards Can Lead to NGFMs

In our member survey, we sought to elicit investor views on whether particular recognition and measurement requirements contributed to NGFMs. The survey results (**Table 2.1**) and accompanying comments provide a high-level indicator of ways in which investors disagree with aspects or find limited usefulness in the reporting outcomes of accounting requirements. Hence, we are not interpreting these particular member results as implying that specific recognition and measurement requirements are flawed in their entirety.

We recognize that specific standards (e.g., revenue recognition and business combinations) are multi-faceted, as they must be in order to apply to a variety of business models and

[16]One key desire by many investors is for information that helps them forecast earnings and cash flows. Investors who understand GAAP and its intended broad standardization, so to speak, may agree with the accounting but find that it is not what they need for forecasting purposes.
[17]See Dichev et al. (2015).

transactions, both simple and complex. Financial statement users could consider accounting standards that are meant to apply to multiple scenarios as failing to adequately reflect the economics of particular transactions or contracts. In other words, these findings might simply reflect an inherent shortcoming of general purpose accounting standards.

That being said, the results (Table 2.1) also point to areas in which standard setters probably need to conduct outreach to investors and identify specific accounting principles or implementation practices that may be generating investors' disagreement with the economic relevance of particular reporting outcomes.

Table 2.1. Recognition and Measurement Requirements Contribute to NGFM

	Agree	Disagree	Not Sure
Business combinations	64.9%	19.2%	15.9%
Intangible assets	63.0%	20.8%	16.1%
Goodwill	57.2%	28.9%	13.9%
Financial instruments	52.9%	23.7%	23.4%
Post-employment	47.0%	30.4%	22.6%
Share-based payments	46.9%	35.5%	17.6%
Revenue recognition	41.0%	43.0%	15.9%
Research and development	36.8%	40.5%	22.6%
Inventory	32.2%	44.6%	23.2%

2.2.4. Offsetting the Aggregate Effects of Conservatism Bias

Young (2013) posits that another plausible explanation for companies reporting NGFMs could be that the aggregate effects of a conservatism bias possibly result in GAAP/IFRS accounting profit being understated relative to economic profit. Hence, there is a perceived need for an upward adjustment of the GAAP/IFRS performance measure.

NGFMs tend to be upward biased relative to GAAP/IFRS measures because they are predominantly calculated by excluding some of the losses and expenses that the GAAP/

IFRS number includes.[18] One argument could be that NGFMs might be reported by companies in an attempt to present a truer picture of economic profit relative to a downwardly biased and conservative GAAP/IFRS performance measure.

How does conservatism bias come into play in a manner that possibly understates accounting profit relative to economic profit? Across specific accounting standards, there is a lower threshold for recognizing losses and liabilities relative to that for recognizing gains and assets. The conservatism bias is reflected in certain asset recognition requirements. For example, unlike acquired intangible assets, internally generated intangible assets are usually not recognized on the balance sheet.

Furthermore, Dechow and Schrand (2004), citing empirical evidence by Penman and Zhang (2002), provide several examples of accounting conservatism in expense recognition that distorts the reflection of the true economic profit in any reporting period, such as the following situations:

- R&D costs are expensed immediately, but the benefits (e.g., increased sales or reduced process costs) are accrued in later years. Hence, accounting profit will be lower than the economic profit in the early years of R&D and higher in later years. If a company has a business model with sustained R&D costs, then its "accelerated" write-down of these costs could consistently yield an accounting profit that is lower than the economic profit. In similar fashion, Lev and Gu (2016) argue that the income statement recognition of restructuring costs does not necessarily match the economic benefits associated with restructuring activities, and this effectively lowers the earnings quality of reporting entities.[19]
- Advertising costs are expensed immediately and, similar to R&D, the benefits of advertising spent are realized mainly in later years.

Companies might not be adjusting the above-stated and arguably conservative R&D or advertising expenses when calculating NGFMs. Yet, if they perceive that their summary performance measures understate the economic profit, companies may be inclined

[18]Gains are also excluded, but on balance, NGFMs tend to be upward adjusted relative to GAAP/IFRS measures. Two other data points prove the upward bias. First, Holland, Kernan, Verdes, and Joseph (2014) reported that in 2012–2013, 79% of FTSE 100 companies reported an adjusted operating profit that was higher than the unadjusted operating profit. Second, a sample of 380 S&P 500 companies reported a 2015 6.6% growth in non-GAAP profit and yet had an 11% decline in GAAP profit (Ciesielski 2016).

[19]Lev and Gu (2016) cite examples where announcements of restructuring costs led to positive capital market reactions. These examples include RBS in February 2013 with $1.7 billion, Pfizer in January 2013 with $943 million, and General Electric in July 2013 with $632 million.

or incentivized to make other adjustments that result in a net upward adjustment of the GAAP/IFRS measure.

The objective of negating a perceived "conservatism bias" of GAAP/IFRS requirements, which disallow the recognition of internally generated intangible assets, could also explain why many companies exclude the amortization or impairment of acquired intangible assets when determining "adjusted net income." In other words, companies could be choosing to ignore the write-down of some portion of recognized intangible assets because they do not recognize the full portfolio of intangible asset amounts (internally generated and acquired) on the balance sheet. Some financial statement preparers may be wondering, why write off a portion of assets when the company cannot recognize another portion of similar assets?

Another example of conservatism bias within the accounting framework is the requirement to write-down or recognize the impairment of long-lived assets whenever there is evidence that the carrying value on the balance sheet is not recoverable. But there is a restriction on writing up assets, including circumstances in which there is a recovery in the value of previously impaired assets.[20]

Finally, it is important to clarify that we are only hypothesizing conservatism bias as a factor that explains why companies may produce NGFMs. We are not suggesting that such reasoning justifies NGFMs from an investor perspective, nor did we explicitly seek member views on the economic relevance or accuracy of GAAP/IFRS measures versus NGFMs.

2.3. Presentation of Primary Financial Statements

We examine key considerations for developing a robust performance framework, including defining performance and enhancing the presentation structure of primary financial statements.

2.3.1. Defining Performance

Within the accounting conceptual framework and standard-setting landscape, there has been a long-running and unresolved debate between two schools of thought on how to best represent performance within financial statements. One approach entails the "all-inclusive

[20]US GAAP generally entirely restricts write-ups of long-lived assets, whereas IFRS can allow write-ups but only to the extent of reversing previously recognized impairments.

income" concept, whereby net income ought to reflect the effects of all periodic changes in shareholders' equity other than transactions with owners. This approach accords importance to the balance sheet and considers that changes to balance sheet assets and liabilities ought to be reflected in the aggregate performance measure (i.e., net income). An alternative approach is the current operating concept predicated on the primacy of income from operating activities. Such income is considered to be sustainable, easier to predict, and controllable by management. Proponents of the current operating concept take the view that earnings should not be distorted by abnormal, non-recurring events and transitory gains or losses.

There are polarized views on the best representation of performance across different stakeholders and different countries. Hence, there has been no consensus with regard to either of these two possible approaches. Instead, the current financial statement presentation requirements blend both approaches, as evidenced by the existence of effectively "two income statements," of which the OCI statement is a separate portion after the net income subtotal.[21]

The net income subtotal itself is an ad hoc amalgamation of items with varied economic characteristics (e.g., gains or losses from trading financial instruments, one-off special items, and inconsistently defined earnings from operating activities). Items reported in OCI tend to be ad hoc and seem primarily aimed at minimizing net income volatility (Papa and Peters 2015).

The absence of a performance reporting framework that is acceptable to all stakeholders contributes to the need for NGFMs. Most notable, some NGFM calculation adjustments are consistent with the derivation of an earnings figure equivalent to notions of "current operating income" and "core earnings." Some NGFM adjustments have the following characteristics:

- Transitory (e.g., financial instruments' fair value and pension re-measurements)
- Non-recurring (e.g., discontinued operations gains or losses, one-off sales)
- Perceived as not being under management's control (e.g., foreign currency adjustments)

Making adjustments for items that are transitory, non-recurring, or not under management control aligns with what many CFOs and capital market participants consider

[21]One could argue that it is effectively two statements, even though OCI is presented as a continuation of the overall comprehensive income statement.

high-quality earnings (Brown, Call, Clement, and Sharp 2015; Dichev, Graham, Harvey, and Rajgopal 2015).

2.3.2. Presentation and Classification Structure of Income Statement and Cash Flow Statement

In the context of today's reporting requirements, the income statement and cash flow statement presentation structure can still result in obfuscation by companies and lack of clarity by investors regarding the components of core performance or cash flow generated from operating activities. For instance, International Accounting Standard (IAS) 1 has very open-ended and principles-based presentation requirements that can be applied quite differently by similar reporting companies.[22] We elaborate further on these perceived shortcomings.

Income Statement Requirements

As **Figure 2.1** shows, different variants of adjusted earnings or operating profit are of interest to investors. Both US GAAP and IFRS have dispensed with a distinction between "below the line" (extraordinary or unusual) and "above the line" items. This hitherto-required distinction may have to some extent helped investors to distinguish among different earnings components. Companies were also often misrepresenting recurring items as extraordinary, however, to the extent that it was necessary to eliminate the boundary.

Cash Flow Statement Requirements

As Figure 2.1A and Figure 2.1B show, free cash flow and its variants are some of the most commonly used NGFMs. Free cash flow is often derived by adjusting the cash from the operating activities subtotal. The presented cash flow from operating activities necessitates several adjustments to yield comparable measures of cash flow–generating abilities across entities. Unlike with the balance sheet and income statement, however, enhancing the statement of cash flows has been a relatively neglected undertaking and not a focal point of standard-setting activities.

[22]IAS 1 states that financial statements must report the information needed to fairly present a company's financial performance, financial position, and changes in cash flows.

Figure 2.1A. Commonly Used NGFMs, "Top-Half"

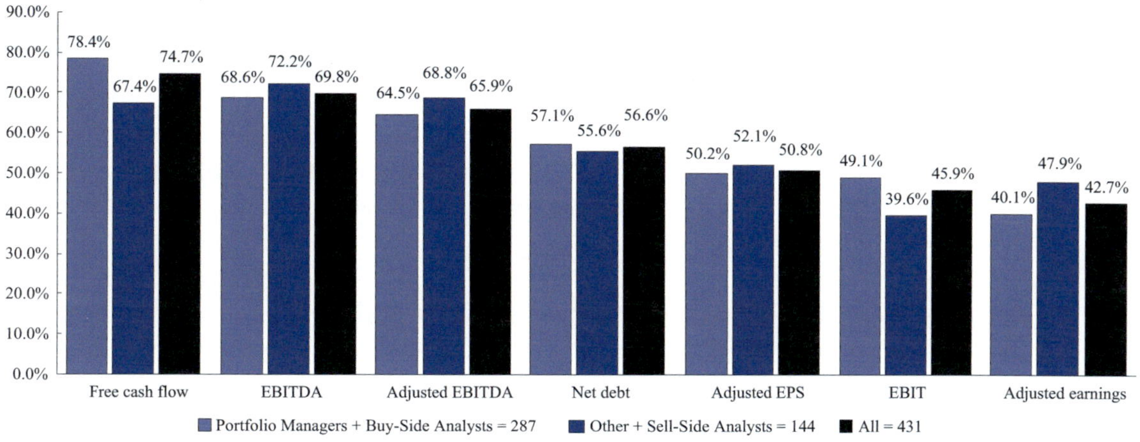

Figure 2.1B. Commonly Used NGFMs, "Bottom-Half"

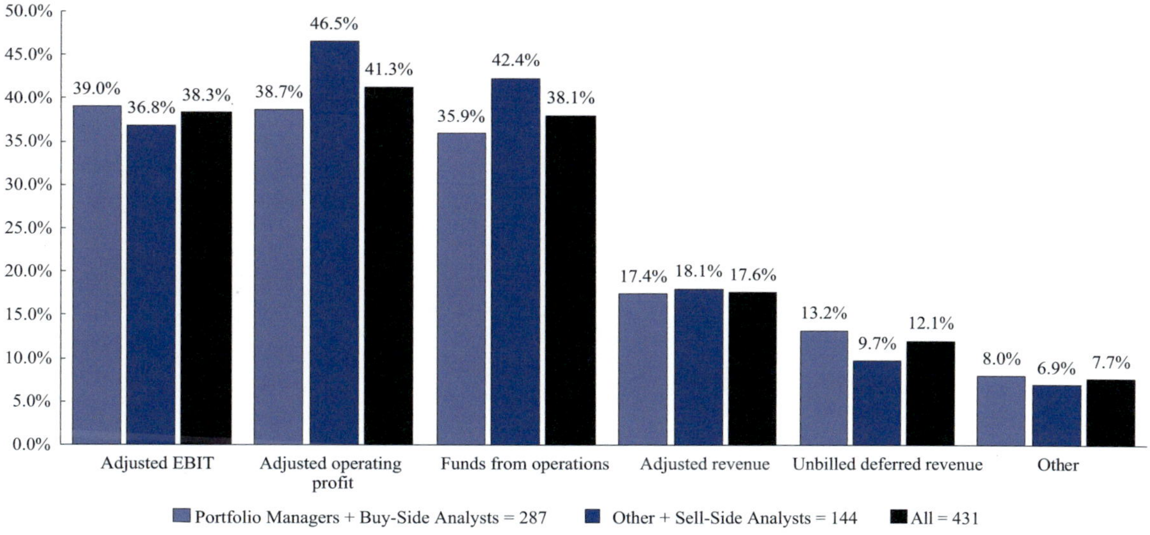

2.4. Conclusion

In this section, we have highlighted challenges with both recognition and measurement requirements as well as with the presentation of primary financial statements that could be motivating the communication of certain types of NGFMs by companies. The two major global accounting standard-setting bodies (the IASB and the FASB) have acknowledged the interplay between NGFM reporting and existing accounting standard performance reporting definitions and requirements, or lack thereof. Speeches by IASB Chair Hans Hoogervorst in 2015 and 2016 and similar pronouncements by FASB board members Tom Linsmeier (whose term recently expired) and Marc Siegel have acknowledged this linkage.

It is encouraging that both these standard setters and their representatives have signaled the priority of a performance reporting project. In the next section, we lay out investor expectations for standard setters with respect to the enhancement of primary financial statements and provide requirements for discipline in reporting NGFMs within financial statements.

3. Investor Expectations of Standard Setters

In addressing investor expectations of accounting standard setters, we principally concentrate[23] on the need for standard setters to (a) enhance existing financial statement presentation requirements and (b) where applicable, impose discipline around reporting NGFMs/APMs within financial statements.

3.1. Overarching Considerations

There are lessons to be learned from previous attempts at defining performance, including defining components of the income statement and OCI. Standard setters risk becoming entangled in a seemingly unrealizable and likely futile quest to come up with a widely accepted definition of performance, as occurred during the IFRS conceptual framework discussion paper and exposure draft deliberations in 2015. The financial statement presentation (FSP) discussion paper issued prior to 2010 focused on finding better ways of presenting information but also seemed to have hit a stalemate in the development of some of its proposals.[24]

Hence, it is necessary to appropriately scope and prioritize frequently articulated investor information needs to ensure timely and meaningful enhancements to the primary financial statements.

That being said, even with the heightened scrutiny on NGFMs by securities regulators, investors, and media, the enhancement of primary financial statements ought not to be seen as being only about fixing or preempting NGFMs. For starters, it is difficult to come up with any definition of performance or subtotal that guarantees there will never be a

[23]The motivations for recognition and measurement changes typically face a higher threshold of acceptance by standard setters than presentation-related changes. For example, recognition and measurement changes entail a wider set of cost–benefit considerations than presentation-related changes. As noted in the previous section, we recommend that accounting standard setters continue to reach out to investors on areas in which some investors disagree with extant recognition and measurement approaches (e.g., business combination and intangible assets).

[24]The FSP Project explored the principles of cohesiveness and disaggregation (e.g., allocation of line items to different columns on the basis of distinguishing economic characteristics) across financial statements and the direct cash flow statement.

need for alternative views of performance by some reporting entities. Hence, standard setters should *not view financial statement presentation as a narrow-scope project of fixing NGFM-related issues*, and they should still address longstanding questions related to comprehensive income, including the following:

- What is the conceptual or economic nature difference between profit and loss compared with OCI line items?
- Should items be reclassified from OCI to the income statement, and if so, why should this occur?

In addition, some specific principles of the previous 2010 financial statement presentation project and proposed by the CFA Institute comprehensive business reporting model (CFA Institute 2007) are worth retaining, including the following:

- *Disaggregation.* An appropriate disaggregation of comprehensive income line items can facilitate the reporting of economically relevant summary measures.
- *Cohesiveness across main financial statements.* Investors would like there to be a linkage among items classified as operating, investing, and financing across the main financial statements. We recognize that a source of resistance to the cohesiveness principle by some stakeholders resulted from the perceived over-engineering of balance sheet classifications. Nonetheless, investors support the notion of cohesiveness in determining presentation requirements because such an approach can yield rich analytical insights and benefits, such as applying line items from different financial statements as inputs for determining return on operating assets.
- *Roll-forwards of material balance sheet line items.* Roll-forwards can help to enhance transparency across financial statements and strengthen investors' understanding of the stock and flow effects, including acquisition and foreign currency effects on reported balances.

In sum, standard setters should indeed focus on implementable ideas addressing the hot issue of the moment (i.e., NGFMs), but they should not forget or relegate their key role in enhancing foundational, conceptual ideas on performance presentation.

3.2. Enhancement of Primary Financial Statements

3.2.1. Income Statement Enhancement

Investors expect an enhanced presentation of comprehensive income components. Such enhancement includes ensuring a consistent definition of different aspects of performance, sufficient disaggregation, and prominent presentation of all key comprehensive income line items.

Effective disaggregation and consistent definition of subtotals could cater to differences in financial statement users' preferences and analytical needs, enabling different users to focus on the relevant information set for their purposes. In other words, investors who are interested only in "core operating earnings" would have a comparable GAAP/IFRS-based number, whereas those who analyze the comprehensive income total and its various components would also have relatively comparable data across companies.

Our survey results convey the following investor expectations:

- *Definition of subtotals.* **Figure 3.1** shows that a majority of respondents (55.1%) expect standard setters to define key subtotals (operating profit; earnings before interest and tax [EBIT]; and earnings before interest, taxes, depreciation, and amortization [EBITDA]).

Figure 3.1. Need for Definition of Subtotals

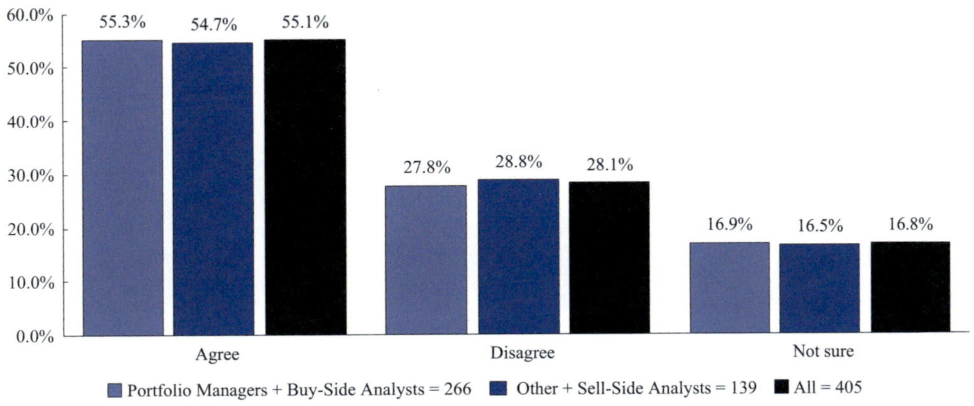

- *Improvement in structure of income statement.* **Figure 3.2** shows that a majority (56.8%) of respondents expect that improvements in the structure of the profit and loss account could reduce the need for NGFMs.

- *Enhanced disaggregation.* **Figure 3.3** shows that most respondents (65.3%) expect that enhanced disaggregation of income statements can reduce the need for NGFMs.

Figure 3.2. Improve the Structure of Profit and Loss

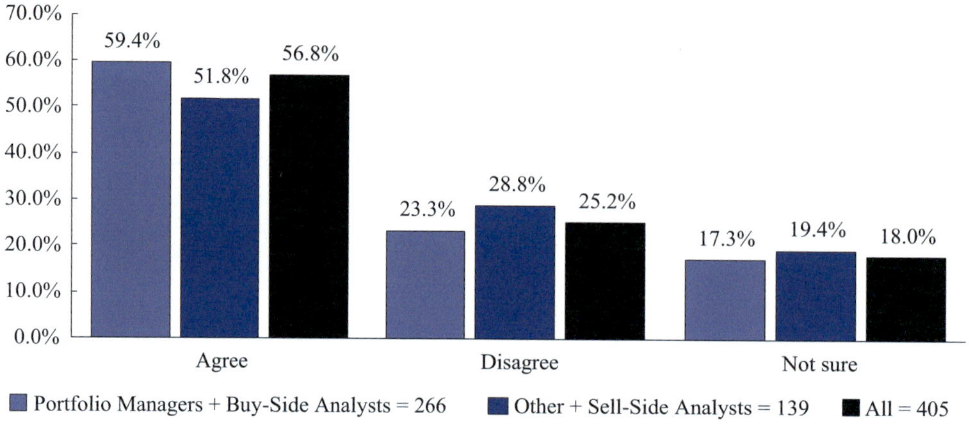

Figure 3.3. Enhance Disaggregation of Income Statements

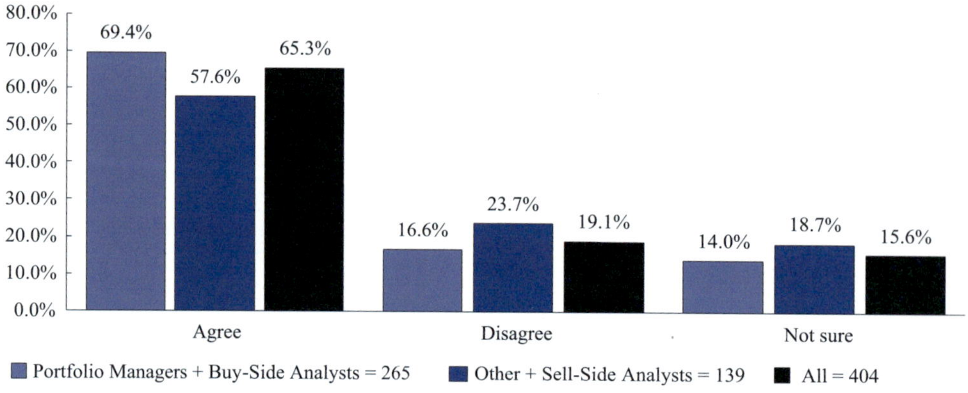

3.2.2. Cash Flow Statement Enhancements

Member survey results (**Figure 3.4**) show support (66.8%) for an enhanced disaggregation and classification of the cash flow statement. Sometimes, there seems to be a bias toward enhancing only the income statement. For investors, however, the cash flow statement is crucial and needs to be addressed too, as emerges clearly from our member survey. This finding is not surprising, because free cash flow is one of the most commonly used NGFMs.

Figure 3.4. Enhance Disaggregation and Classification of Cash Flow Statements

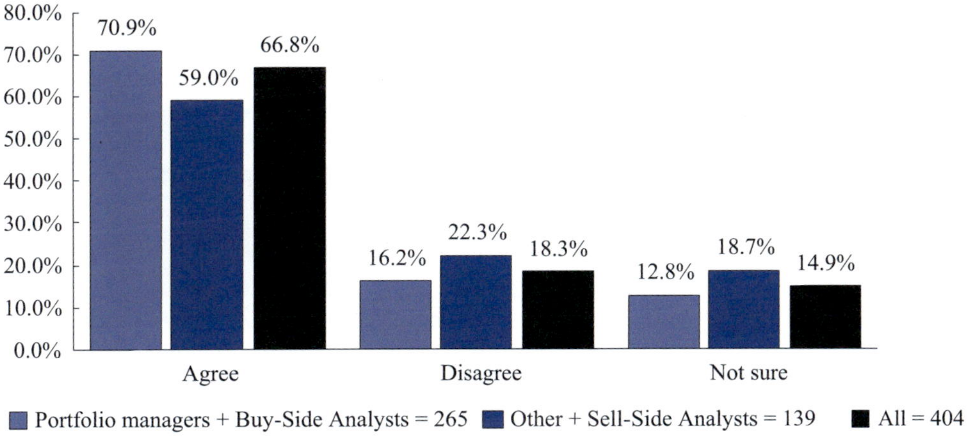

3.3. Discipline around Reporting NGFMs/APMs within Financial Statements

The role of standard setters in ensuring consistency and reliability of NGFMs/APMs arises when these measures can be reported within financial statements (e.g., for IFRS reporting jurisdictions) and are outside the scope of securities regulators' guidelines (e.g., IOSCO and ESMA). In a more general sense, member survey results (**Figure 3.5**) show that capital market participants expect accounting standard setters to provide guidance related to NGFMs (according to 65.5% of respondents).

Figure 3.5. Views on Accounting Standard Setter Guidance Related to NGFMs

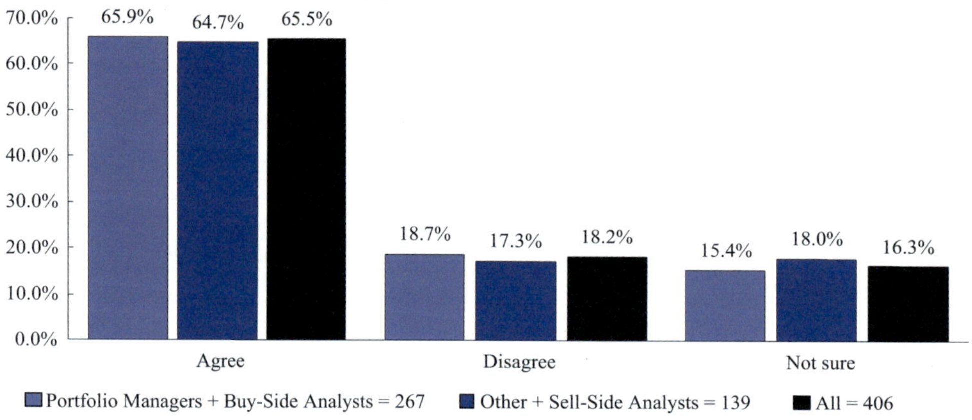

The following member respondent comment reflects many investors' expectations for standard setters:

> *The absence of standards on the definition of key items in the income statement and inadequate disaggregation has created a vacuum in which APMs have proliferated. Time for standard setters to re-impose some discipline. —Respondent*

Another member survey data point that highlights expectations for an increased role by accounting standard setters relates to expectations for NGFMs' location. The findings (**Figure 3.6**) show that 51.2% of respondents prefer NGFMs to be reported either within the primary financial statements (19.2%) or in the notes to the primary financial statements (32.0%) and, by implication, to be under the purview of accounting standard setters.

The IASB has had NGFM/APM-related deliberations while discussing the fair presentation of performance measures in the Principles of Disclosure project. The related 2015 IASB staff paper outlined the following principles:

- IFRS should include additional guidance on the depiction of non-recurring, unusual, or infrequently occurring items in the statement of comprehensive income.

Figure 3.6. Preferred Location of NGFMs

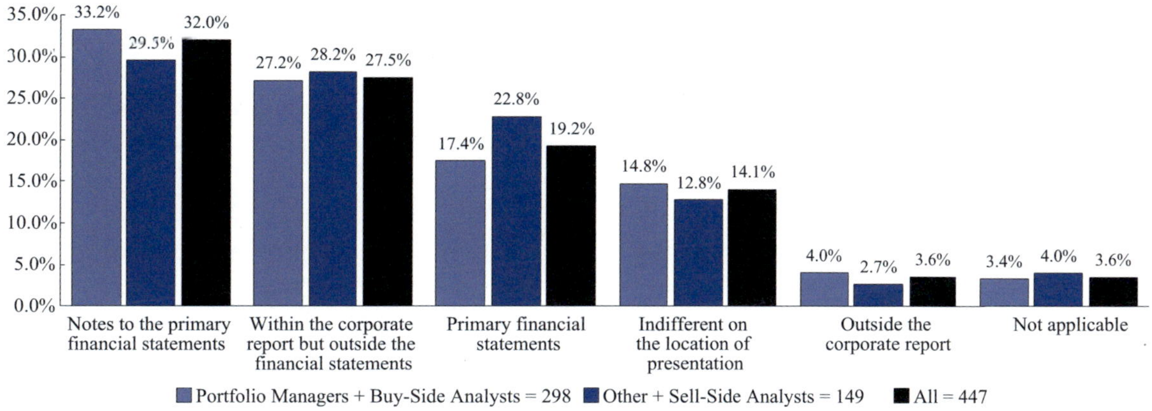

- The presentation of EBIT and EBITDA in the statement of profit or loss complies with IFRS, provided that the statement is presented "by nature" and such subtotals are in accordance with paragraphs 85–85B of IAS 1 *Presentation of Financial Statements*.
- IFRS should not prohibit the disclosure of APMs in the notes to financial statements.

3.4. Conclusion

We recognize the existence of potential conceptual and political challenges toward enhancing the primary financial statement presentation requirements so as to reduce the need for supplemental reporting via NGFMs. For starters, it is difficult to define an operating income subtotal that can be applicable for all industries. Second, there are sometimes deeply entrenched and polarized views on the appropriate representation of performance, and these are likely to remain.

Notwithstanding these obstacles, in this section we have highlighted fairly clear messages on investor expectations around the classification and presentation of the income statement and cash flow statement on which standard setters could focus. Even if they focus on addressing measures associated with current NGFMs, however, we recommend that accounting standard setters should not view the performance reporting project as being only about fixing NGFMs, especially because other types of such measures can always emerge.

4. Assessment of Securities Regulators' Measures

As several securities regulators around the world "up the ante," aiming to rein in NGFM misreporting, it is necessary to consider how effective the regulatory measures already in place are.

Figure 4.1 illustrates the spectrum of possible actions that securities regulators could pursue to encourage effective reporting of NGFMs. To varying degrees, securities regulators across different jurisdictions have aimed to curtail misleading NGFM reporting by applying different aspects of these regulatory levers.

Figure 4.1. Regulatory Levers

4.1. Regulatory Guidelines

4.1.1. Broad Objectives of Guidelines

The SEC, ESMA, and IOSCO have each issued guidelines at different junctures since 2002. Despite differing levels of specificity and restrictiveness, and sometimes applying differing language toward similar areas of redress (e.g., IOSCO and ESMA), these regulatory guidelines share quite similar broad objectives:

- Enhancing the information content of NGFMs

- Ensuring faithful representation of these measures
- Enhancing the measures' comparability and consistency
- Ensuring that undue prominence is not accorded to these measures relative to the most directly comparable GAAP/IFRS number

We next examine these regulators' specific requirements.

4.1.2. US Requirements

US requirements consist of the following:

- Regulation G, enacted in 2003 after Sarbanes–Oxley, is relevant for regulatory filings, press releases, and other management communications.
- Item 10(e) guides reporting of NGFMs under Regulation S-K requirements—all filings with SEC under the Securities Act and the Exchange Act.
- Item 12 guides reporting of NGFMs in Form 8-K.

Figure 4.2 summarizes key aspects of US SEC guidelines concerning NGFMs.

Figure 4.2. US Guidelines on NGFMs

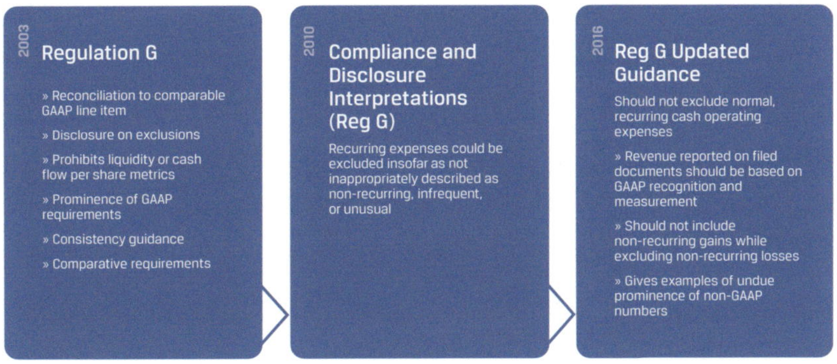

4.1.3. IOSCO and ESMA Guidelines

Outside the United States, IOSCO and ESMA have issued guidelines that target the same areas of deficiency in NGFM reporting as those addressed by the SEC. These guidelines are less prescriptive (e.g., on undue prominence) as well as less restrictive concerning acceptable locations for reporting these adjusted performance and liquidity measures. Other jurisdictions (e.g., Australia, Canada, South Africa, and the United Kingdom) have guidelines too, but we limit our analysis to the three mentioned regulators whose span of influence is fairly global (i.e., SEC, IOSCO, and ESMA).

Scope

Both IOSCO and ESMA's guidance is intended for NGFMs/APMs disclosed outside the IFRS financial statements and notes, including press releases; periodic reports, including management's discussion and analysis (MD&A) or operating and financial review (OFR); disclosure documents filed with securities regulators and stock exchanges; and other communications to shareholders and market participants. ESMA's guidelines do not apply to APMs presented in an entity's financial statements.

Composition of Guidelines

IOSCO, which first issued a cautionary statement on the use of NGFMs in May 2002, updated its guidance in June 2016. Similarly, ESMA's guidelines on APMs took effect in July 2016 following a consultative process that began in 2014 and aimed to build on guidelines by ESMA's predecessor body, the Committee of European Securities Regulators (CESR).

Table 4.1 delineates the areas addressed by these guidelines. ESMA guidelines largely overlap those of IOSCO, even when applying differing language for similar principles (e.g., define, label, explain, reconcile, have comparatives, prominence).

As the delineation in Table 4.1 shows, ESMA and IOSCO principles largely overlap except that ESMA does not explicitly include in its guidelines the following two IOSCO principles:

- Unbiased principle (should not use non-GAAP measures to avoid presenting adverse information)
- Explicit caution against comparing NGFMs across companies

Table 4.1. IOSCO and ESMA Guidelines

Broad Category	Guidelines and Principles
Define	IOSCO: Define the non-GAAP financial measure and provide a clear explanation of the basis of calculation. ESMA: Define APMs used as well as basis of calculation.
Label	IOSCO: Label the measures clearly as non-GAAP in a way that they are distinguished from GAAP measures. ESMA: Label NGFM and adjustments appropriately. ESMA gives examples of appropriate labels (e.g., not to use overly optimistic or positive labels, such as "protected returns;" not to use labels defined in the applicable financial reporting framework that are confusingly similar when referring to APMs; or not to mislabel items as non-recurring, infrequent, or unusual).
Explicit caution against comparison across companies	IOSCO: Explicitly state that NGFM does not have standardized meaning prescribed by the issuer's GAAP and therefore may not be comparable to similar measures presented by other issuers.
Explain	IOSCO: Explain the reason for presenting NGFMs, including why they are useful to investors and for what additional purposes, if any, management uses the measures. ESMA: Explain why an issuer believes the presentation of APMs provides useful information to users regarding the financial position, cash flows, and results of the operations.
Unbiased	IOSCO: Should not use non-GAAP measures to avoid presenting adverse information.
Prominence	IOSCO: Should not present non-GAAP financial measures with more prominence than the most directly comparable GAAP measure. Presentation and accompanying information should not in any way confuse or obscure the presentation of GAAP measures. ESMA: APMs should not be displayed with more prominence, emphasis, or authority than measures stemming directly from financial statements.

(continued)

Table 4.1. IOSCO and ESMA Guidelines (continued)

Broad Category	Guidelines and Principles
Reconcile	IOSCO: • Provide a clear and concise quantitative reconciliation from non-GAAP to most directly comparable GAAP measure. • Reconciling items derived in the GAAP financial information should be reconcilable to the financial statements. If not extracted from financial statement, reconciliation should show how this figure is calculated. ESMA: • Give a reconciliation of the APMs to the most directly reconcilable line item, subtotal, or total presented in the financial statements. • Where reconciling items are included in financial statements, users should be able to identify them in those financial statements. When a reconciling item cannot be extracted directly from the financial statements, the reconciliation should show how the figure is calculated.
Comparability across periods	IOSCO: • Provide non-GAAP measures for comparative periods. • Non-GAAP financial measures should be presented consistently from period to period. ESMA: • Provide comparatives for the corresponding previous periods. • Unless there are good reasons for change, presentation of APMs should be consistent over time.
Recurring items	IOSCO: Restructuring costs and asset impairments should not be described as non-recurring, infrequent, or unusual without sufficient explanation. ESMA: As described under the "label" caption, ESMA guidelines are that companies should not mislabel items as non-recurring, infrequent, or unusual (e.g., restructuring costs that affected past periods and will affect future periods).
Access to associated information	IOSCO: Associated information should accompany the NGFM, or a reference should be provided as to where such information is available.

Sources: ESMA (2015), IOSCO (2016), and Deloitte (2016).

Another important difference between these two guidelines is that only ESMA guidelines have legal status and require companies to which they pertain to make every effort to comply with the guidelines. ESMA guidelines are addressed to EU country supervisors, and most have indicated that they have incorporated these into their supervisory practices and are expected to monitor application.

4.1.4. Effectiveness of Regulatory Guidelines

Even with the latest round of SEC, ESMA, and IOSCO updates, it is fair to say that regulators are still searching for the "golden mean" in terms of determining how to effectively rein in the misleading reporting of NGFMs. Several academic studies have assessed the effectiveness of regulatory guidelines, albeit with a focus on US 2003 Regulation G requirements. We are unaware of any studies that assess the effect of regulatory guidelines outside the United States, however, including the IOSCO guidelines, which were first issued in 2002.

Existing academic evidence shows an improvement in the quality of NGFM reporting by US filers after SEC Regulation G guidance took effect in 2003. Regulation G's guidance included the need for reconciliation of NGFMs to the most directly comparable GAAP line item, enhanced disclosure of NGFM choice and calculation, and restrictions on excluding recurring expenses in NGFM calculations. This guidance led to greater overall transparency and a reduced frequency of companies reporting NGFMs. The evidence shows that many companies that had low-quality exclusions prior to the enactment of Regulation G stopped communicating NGFMs when the guidance became effective.

The evidence also shows, however, that the 2003 Regulation G requirements contributed to companies shifting recurring expenses to special items, as well as to a decline in information quality of exclusions for some companies (Kolev, Marquardt, and McVay 2008).

The SEC issued C&DI effective from 2010, superseding the Regulation G requirements. The 2010 C&DI relaxed the prohibitions on excluding recurring expenses, clarifying that recurring expenses could be excluded insofar as they are not inappropriately described as non-recurring, infrequent, or unusual.

We are unaware of any academic empirical evidence assessing the effect of the 2010 updates on NGFM quality and quantity along the same lines as studies assessing the effect of the 2003 Regulation G guidelines. However, as observed in Marcogliese and Kim (2016), the 2010 Regulation G C&DI seems to have relaxed the restrictions in NGFM reporting and contributed to the following trends:

- Increases in the type and frequency of NGFM calculation adjustments
- The relaxation of NGFM reporting requirements for foreign filers

In sum, from the US experience, it appears that too-tight regulatory constraints on exclusions in NGFM calculations can lower the incremental information content of adjustments that are labeled as special items. For example, recurring line items can end up being mislabeled as special items. Yet, too-lax requirements result in a higher frequency of both recurring and non-recurring exclusions in NGFM calculations, as seems to be the case after the issuance of the 2010 C&DI.

Our survey results (**Figure 4.3**) show that only 15.7% of respondents consider existing regulatory guidelines to be adequate. In part, it is unlikely that many investors are familiar with the fine print of different regulatory guidelines. Even when ESMA and IOSCO have held a consultative process, the rate of comment letter responses has been low.[25]

Figure 4.3. Investor Perceptions on Adequacy of Regulatory Guidelines

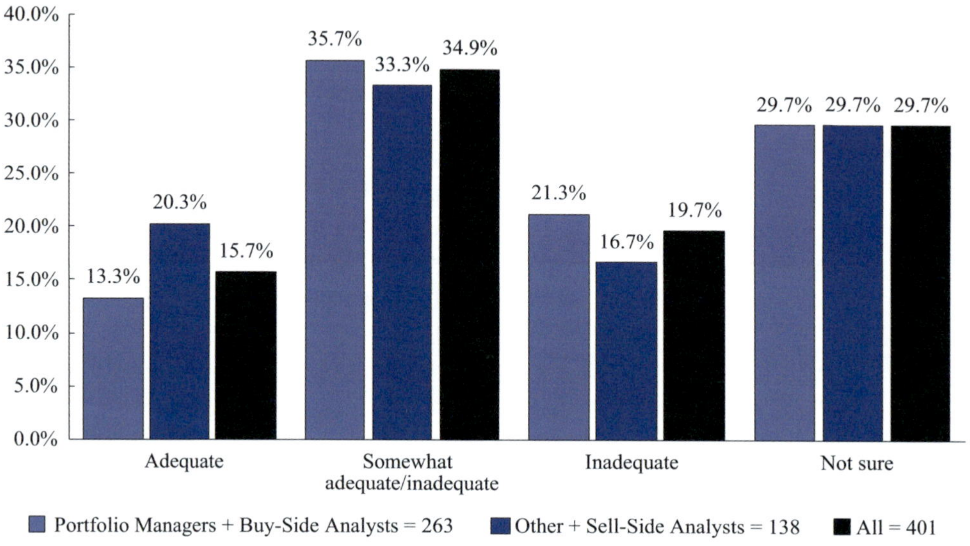

[25]IOSCO's 2014 consultation on non-GAAP measures had only 21 institutional responses, with 2 from investor representatives.

This finding of low perceived adequacy of guidelines could also be correlated with difficulties in investors observing regulatory monitoring actions, as well as the fact that there has barely been any enforcement. The following survey results further show that respondents consider monitoring and enforcement actions to be similarly inadequate.

4.2. Regulatory Monitoring and Enforcement Actions

Among the global regulators, only the US SEC has made publicly available a quantified articulation of the regulatory efforts and outcomes of monitoring companies' reporting of NGFMs (i.e., comment letters). **Table 4.2** profiles SEC comment letters issued to firms that had IPOs. One can observe a rise in both the number of IPOs that use NGFMs and the percentage of IPOs that received a comment letter.

Table 4.2. Profile of Comment Letters

Year	IPOs That Used Non-GAAP Metrics	IPOs That Received Non-GAAP Comment Letters	Percentage of IPOS That Received Non-GAAP Comment Letters	IPOs That Received Follow-Up Non-GAAP Comment Letters	Percentage of IPOS That Received Follow-Up Non-GAAP Comment Letters
2010	56	35	63%	11	31%
2011	67	39	58	15	38
2012	76	31	41	8	26
2013	113	58	51	12	21
2014*	127	52	41	4	8
Total	439	215	49%	50	23%

*2014 represents a partial year, from January to November.
Source: www.auditanalytics.com/blog/use-of-non-gaap-metrics-in-ipo-prospectuses-sec-comment-letters

In contrast to mandatory GAAP/IFRS information, NGFMs' voluntary nature makes it harder for securities regulators to pursue enforcement actions for misreporting of these alternative measures. Nonetheless, it still seems odd that there has been only one enforcement action (SafeNet in 2009), despite the Regulation G guidelines having been in place for more than 10 years as well as a rising frequency of comment letters issued to companies in the last few years. For instance, NGFMs were the fourth-highest source of comment letters in 2015 (Deloitte 2015).

Given that the United States is widely seen as having the world's most robust capital market regulatory oversight regime, it is reasonable to expect that other global regulators may face similar challenges in pursuing enforcement actions in their jurisdictions.

Our survey results (**Figures 4.4** and **4.5**) show that very few investors consider regulators' monitoring and enforcement measures to be adequate.[26]

Figure 4.4. Perceived Adequacy of Regulators Monitoring and Engaging Companies

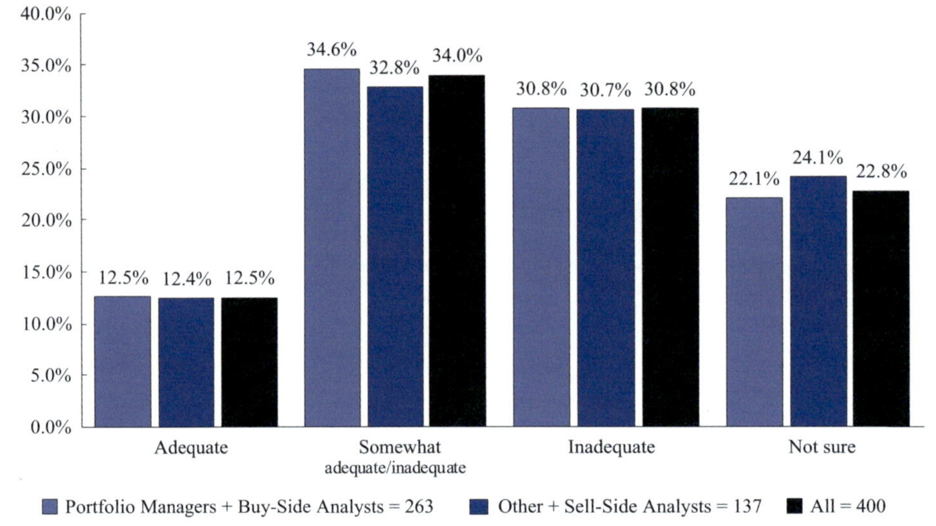

[26]As noted, we are aware of a quantified articulation of monitoring efforts by the US SEC only. Hence, it is possible that the poor rating of adequacy of monitoring actions reflects the inclusion of respondents from across the globe.

Figure 4.5. Perceived Adequacy of Regulator Enforcement Actions on Misleading NGFMs

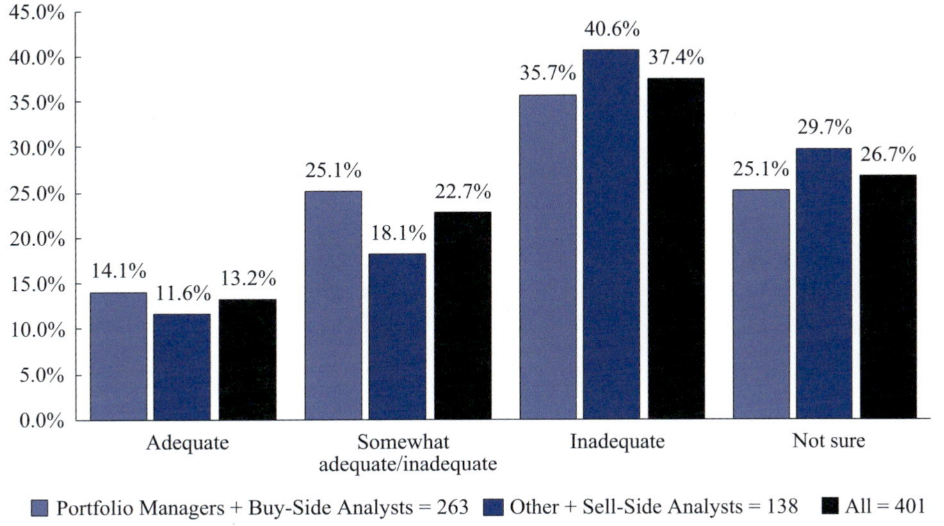

Various comments from survey respondents reveal that investors expect tougher and more-observable actions from regulators:

> *It's clear to me that some companies are now showing abusive behavior in the use of the NGFMs that actively misrepresent their true financial condition. I have seen cases of uncovered dividends being made to look covered; apparently profitable companies actually struggling to cover their interest payments. Regulation could perhaps target the most clearly abusive cases, such as recurring cash items that are essential costs of doing business being treated as non-core. Some items are rendered meaningless by adjustments. What, in economic terms, is a "non-core" tax rate? Companies would not benefit from all of the deductions that they do if their profitability was really so much higher. I have had one company's CFO describe "Core Tax" as a completely made-up number.... Perhaps banning non-GAAP measures below the PBT [profit before tax] level would help.*
>
> —Respondent

> *Management teams are often being overly aggressive. Adjustments often not justifiable. Regulators need to put some fear into management. Management should think*

long and hard before making adjustments. Aggressive behavior should be called out and punished.

—Respondent

Many companies, especially in "tech," should essentially be valued at about zero if regulators were doing their jobs with respect to true accounting reporting accuracy.

—Respondent

Companies need to be held to the same standards on NGFM as they are with GAAP, especially as they trumpet them so and often CEO comp is based on them.

—Respondent

SEC let the genie out of the bottle in 2003. Has done little to encourage better behavior, only worsened it in 2010 with their C&DI.

—Respondent

"Everyone's doing it," and I don't think the genie can be put back in the bottle, and frankly many of the adjustments help to create comparable financial statements across time and to get an understanding of the underlying business performance, so quite simply there [needs] to be a somewhat standardized disclosure regarding these adjustments. Some companies are responsible with these adjustments, but some take a "kitchen sink" approach and should be discouraged from doing so.

—Respondent

SEC requirements on GAAP versus non-GAAP are rarely enforced.

—Respondent

4.3. Conclusion

Regulators in different jurisdictions have fulfilled a restraining role by providing the guidelines of what is acceptable, and the SEC has observable evidence of monitoring company reporting (i.e., comment letters).

The sense remains, however, that regulators need to bite a lot more than they have barked if they are to be involved in the NGFM space, as they have become by issuing a raft of guidelines. In the next section, we highlight investor expectations on specific regulatory guidelines.

5. Investor Expectations on Regulatory Requirements

In the previous section, we conveyed that investors expect more discernible proof of different regulatory measures, translating to improved corporate reporting behavior. In this section, we highlight investor expectations on different specific regulatory requirements.

5.1. Currently Reported Reconciliation and Disclosures

Table 5.1 (also reported in Part 1 of this publication) highlights the perceived adequacy of different components of NGFM information.

From the foregoing results, there is a need for securities regulators to emphasize and continue to monitor the following:

- Investors' ready access to NGFM information (adequacy of signposting)
- Quality of disclosures on adjustments and explanation for using NGFMs
- Reconciliation quality, including choice of directly comparable GAAP/IFRS line items and an appropriate level of disaggregation in the reconciliation

There is also scope to specify and require disclosures that can enhance comparability and reconciliation of the same NGFM across companies.

Table 5.1. Views on Adequacy of Reconciliations and Disclosures

	Adequate	Sometimes Adequate/ Inadequate	Inadequate	Not Sure
Comparability across Periods				
Year-to-year comparatives**	30.7%	45.1%	17.8%	6.4%
Reconciliations				
Signposting and location of reconciliations within the annual reports and/or other management communication documents*	24.4%	40.0%	26.7%	8.8%
Management choice of the most directly comparable GAAP/ IFRS line item**	22.2%	50.2%	16.5%	11.1%
Disaggregation of adjustments in the reconciliation to the most directly comparable GAAP/ IFRS line item**	28.5%	43.7%	19.0%	8.8%
Disclosures				
Explanations for using particular NGFMs/APMs*	24.7%	45.5%	24.2%	5.7%
Contextual information, explanation, and economic reasons provided for the chosen NGFMs' related adjustments*	23.4%	38.5%	31.3%	6.8%
Disclosures that can enable the reconciliation and comparison of different NGFMs that are communicated by similar companies*	21.5%	39.4%	31.2%	7.9%

*A higher proportion of respondents found this reconciliation or disclosure component to be inadequate than those who found it adequate.

**A higher proportion of respondents found this reconciliation or disclosure component to be adequate than those who found it inadequate.

5.2. Investor Views on a Selection of Regulatory Requirements

5.2.1. Investor Views on Prohibition of Certain NGFMs in Filed Documents

The survey results (**Figures 5.1** and **5.2**) show that only 37.3% of respondents agree with prohibiting non-GAAP revenue within filed regulatory documents, and 10.8% agree with prohibiting the cash flow and liquidity per share metrics. These prohibitions were conveyed in the SEC 2016 C&DI. The results probably point to a need for the commission to reach out to investors and validate areas of concern.

Figure 5.1. Non-GAAP Revenue within Filed Regulatory Documents

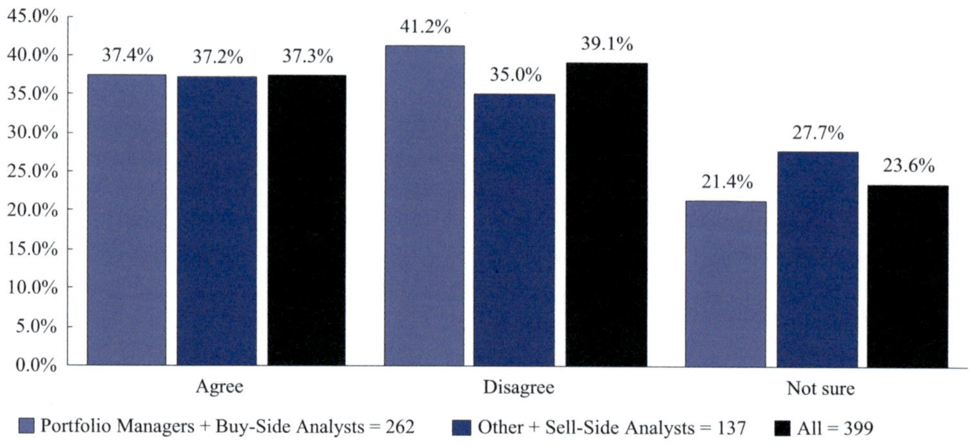

Figure 5.2. Cash Flow and Liquidity per Share Metrics within Filed Documents

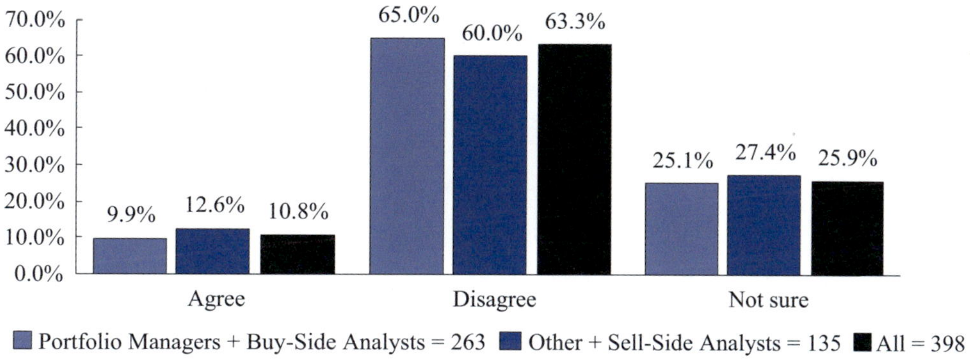

5.2.2. Investor Views on NGFM Calculation Restraints

In Part 1 of this publication, we highlighted that a majority of investors consider it usually inappropriate to exclude recurring expenses in NGFM calculations. The survey results (**Figures 5.3** and **5.4**) show investor support for prohibiting NGFM adjustments that bias the view of performance (i.e., excluding recurring expenses and cherry picking gains).

Figure 5.3. Prohibiting Exclusion of Recurring Expenses

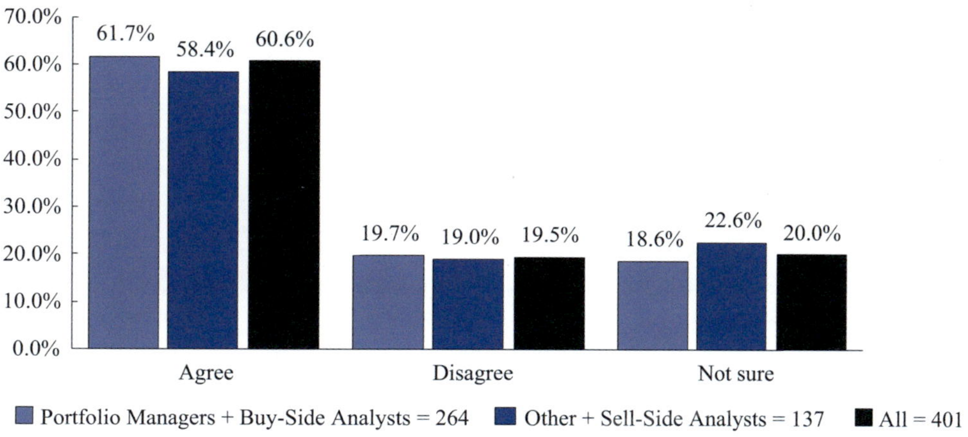

Figure 5.4. Inclusion of Non-Recurring Gains while Excluding Similar Losses

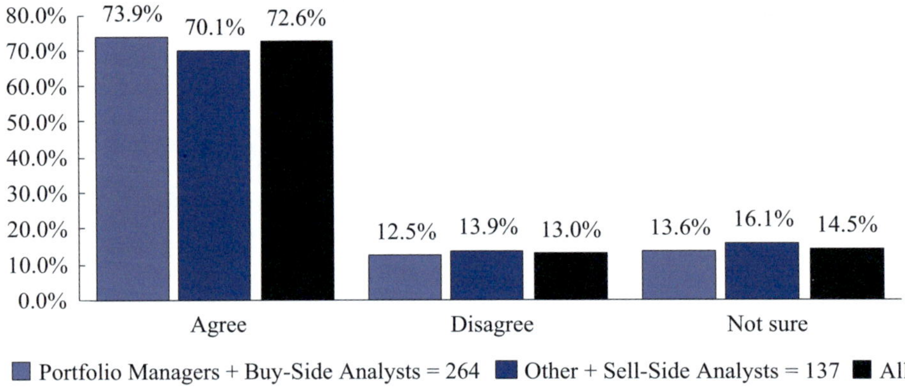

5.2.3. Investor Views on NGFM Reconciliation Enhancements

Member survey results (**Figure 5.5**) reveal strong support (66.1%) for the disaggregation of tax effects of NGFMs as required by the SEC 2016 C&DI. In general, investors tend to prefer gross as opposed to net presentation of line items and intra-tax allocation because such disaggregation is helpful for analyzing different line item components. Hence, it is unsurprising to discover investor support for the disaggregation of tax effects of NGFMs.

Figure 5.5. Disaggregation of Tax Effects of NGFMs

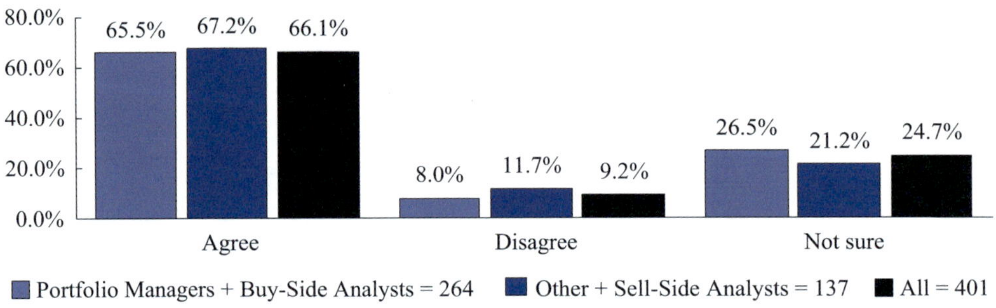

5.2.4. Investor Views on NGFM Location and Undue Prominence

Member survey results (**Figure 5.6**) show a majority support (52.5%) for specific examples of undue prominence of NGFMs. The results (**Figure 5.7**) also show support (71.1%) for including press release NGFMs within regulatory filings, which leads to greater transparency and consistency across multiple management communication channels. **Figure 5.8** shows, however, that there is disagreement (54.4%) about prohibiting NGFMs within audited financial statements.

Figure 5.6. Specific Examples of Undue Prominence Are Necessary

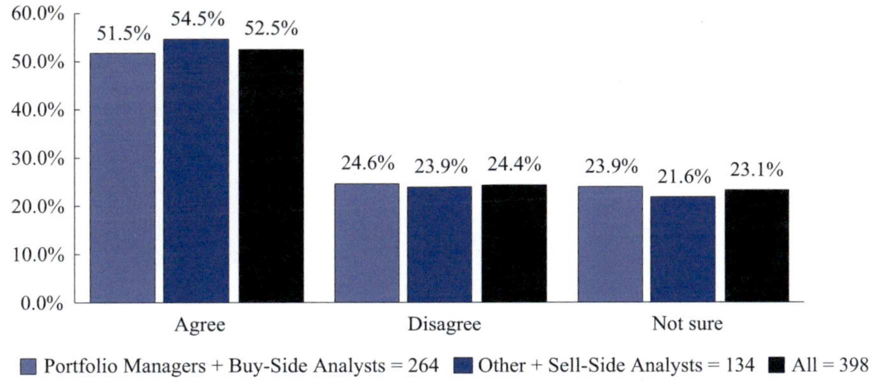

Figure 5.7. Press Release NGFMs Should Be Reported within Regulatory Filings

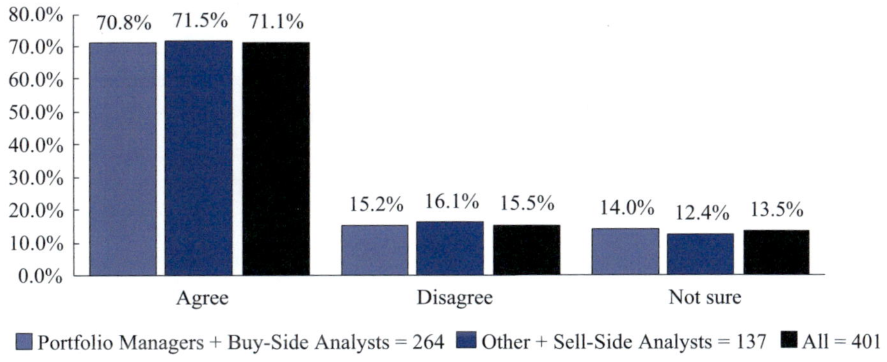

Figure 5.8. NGFMs Should Not Be Included within Audited Financial Statements

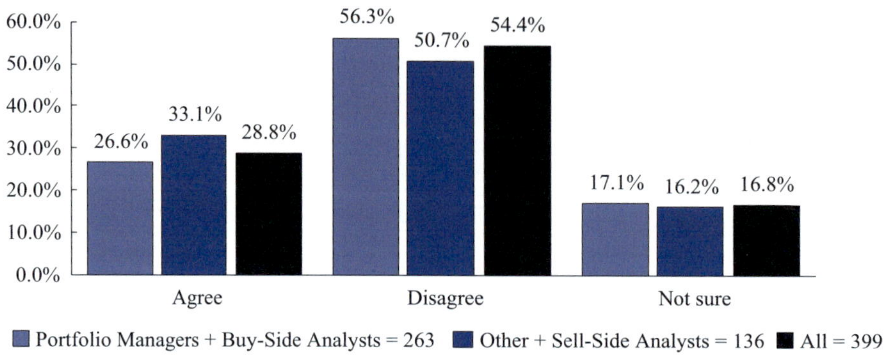

5.3. Conclusion

Investor feedback illustrates a need for securities regulators to emphasize and continue to monitor the information quality of NGFMs conveyed through current requirements of reconciliations and disclosures. There is also scope to specify and require disclosures that can enhance comparability and reconciliation of the same NGFMs across companies.

In addition, significant investor support exists for the emphasis on particular measures that the SEC, IOSCO, and ESMA have respectively enacted—specifically, those measures that (a) preclude exclusion of recurring expenses and (b) cherry pick, by inclusion of certain gains and exclusion of losses of a similar nature in NGFM calculation.

It also seems that many investors are comfortable with NGFMs being included in primary financial statements, although the SEC requirements prohibit this approach. Investors appear to expect a greater level of assurance than currently provided, as we discuss in the next section. Investors are less clear, however, on the purpose or motivation for certain prohibitions (for example, adjusted revenue and cash flow and liquidity per share metrics within filed regulatory documents, as prohibited by the SEC).

Finally, we propose that there may be a role for regulators to go beyond just providing restraining measures and to also pursue a positive reinforcement approach by creating a framework of highlighting and sharing good NGFM reporting practices.

6. Other Expectations: Companies, Audit Committees, Auditors, and Investors

6.1. Company Responsibilities

A PwC (2016) viewpoint paper identifies the following areas on which companies could focus to build confidence in non-GAAP measures and other KPIs:

- *Ensure robust disclosure controls.* Management should ensure the controls and procedures around the calculation and presentation of NGFMs are as robust as those for financial statement information. Management should ensure that NGFMs are reviewed by disclosure committees and the internal audit function. These particular proposals have also been put forward by CAQ (2016) and Aughton and Burns (2016).

- *Aim for NGFMs that are comparable across peers.* Doing so may entail working with industry groups to ensure comparable voluntary measures across peers.

- *Conform to existing and emerging regulatory guidelines around consistency, transparency, and prominence of NGFMs.*

We agree with the previous suggestions and most of all emphasize the need for companies to aim to provide high-quality NGFMs across all platforms, regardless of whether external assurance is provided. We discuss assurance next.

6.2. Role of Audit Committees and Boards of Directors

Those charged with governance in reporting entities, including audit committees, have a critical role to play in ensuring companies are not misleading investors with NGFMs. Academic evidence (Frankel, McVay, and Soliman 2011) shows that the independence of a company's board of directors affects NGFM quality.

The CAQ issued some useful guidelines for audit committees to take an active role in ensuring the transparency, consistency, and comparability of NGFMs. Audit committees should have robust oversight over reported NGFMs. They should also highlight any outcomes of oversight activities regarding NGFMs in their audit committee reports.

Boards of directors should also ensure that executive compensation is not linked to rosier-than-warranted NGFMs in a manner that incentivizes executive management to take disproportionate risks, as discussed in Part 1 of this publication. Corporate governance mechanisms, including performance-based compensation, aim to align managers' interests with those of shareholders. Executive compensation within companies, however, is often based on adjusted performance metrics, and as noted, these metrics can be positively biased and do not always faithfully reflect the reporting entity's economic performance.

6.3. Role of Auditors

We sought to establish investor expectations around the level of assurance on NGFMs. Member survey results (**Figure 6.1**) show that 80.8% of respondents expect some level of assurance on NGFMs.

Figure 6.1. Expectations around NGFM Assurance

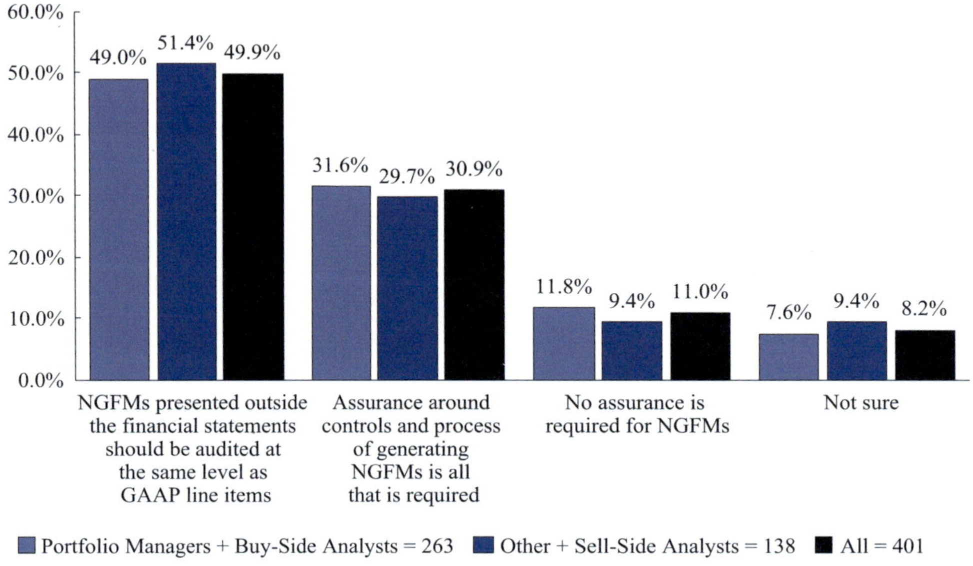

As discussed in Section 1 of this paper, the PCAOB is considering a review of auditors' role and level of assurance required for NGFMs, and several market commentators (e.g., Joshi, Joseph, and Velandy 2014) have also proposed such a review.

The level of assurance depends on location (e.g., press releases versus MD&A versus financial statements). When NGFMs are presented within financial statements, as is allowed under IFRS, they are subject to the full audit requirements. If, however, NGFMs are presented as supplemental information outside the financial statements and annual reports (e.g., in press releases), then auditors need only to ensure that such information is consistent with the knowledge acquired in the audit process.

That being said, the audit standard requirements on supplemental information (e.g., PCAOB Standard 17) do not make it easy for investors to meaningfully assess the extent and quality of assurance, if any, that auditors provide on supplemental information, including NGFMs. From the vantage point of stakeholders outside the audit profession, it could seem that auditors are either effectively applying a lower level of assurance on supplemental information outside the financial statements or ignoring such information entirely—especially in light of the ever-running commentary highlighting seemingly unending episodes of misleading NGFMs.

Different commentators (e.g., Joshi, Joseph, and Velandy 2014) have proposed different ideas for the enhanced role of auditors, including the following:

- Assurance on whether the controls and procedures for calculation and presentation of NGFMs are as robust as those in place for generating financial statement information.
- Assurance on the appropriateness and completeness of items that companies adjust to derive NGFMs. For example, auditors may determine materiality based on what they consider to be core performance. Hence, auditors ought to be able to judge the appropriateness of adjustments made in NGFMs.
- Assurance on compliance with security regulations (e.g., ensuring that there is no inclusion of gains in NGFM that have excluded losses of a similar nature to the gain).

Given the variety of preliminary ideas on possible levels of assurance, there is a need for audit standard setters and auditors to undertake investor outreach to further substantiate investor expectations on the appropriate level of assurance. Such outreach will likely also entail building awareness and eliminating any information and/or expectation gaps that investors may have with respect to either the level or lack of assurance provided for NGFMs.

6.4. Role of Investors and Sell-Side Analysts

Companies provide NGFMs with the intention of meeting investor and financial analyst information needs for valuation purposes. Many investors find NGFMs useful. However, they also often consider certain exclusions made in NGFM calculations to be inappropriate—especially recurring expenses (e.g., stock option expenses). Consequently, as discussed in Section 1 of this paper, sell-side analysts and buy-side investors ought to, when possible, use any platforms of access to company management to actively engage and directly convey their views on any exclusions that they find inappropriate.

Investors also need to push company management for more-comprehensive explanations of why all the chosen adjustments made in calculating NGFMs are considered incrementally informative of the reporting entity's performance. In other words, if there is a growing concern about quality of NGFMs, investors have a duty to have dialogue with and directly push companies for better reporting, even under voluntary reporting regimes.

6.5. Conclusion

In this publication, we have conveyed that multiple factors influence the supply of and demand for NGFMs. Furthermore, NGFMs will likely continue to exist in one form or another.

Concurrently, there is a spread of responsibilities across different market actors for ensuring that only high-quality performance measures (whether mandated or voluntary) are being communicated. In this publication, we have highlighted expectations and potential roles for each key market actor (accounting standard setters, securities regulators, auditors, audit committees, and investors) toward bridging the gap between high-quality (informative and faithfully representative of economics) and low-quality (different but not incrementally informative and/or misleading) NGFMs.

7. References

Aughton, J., and J. Burns. 2016. "Minding the Non-GAAP Measures: How to Establish Disclosure Controls for Non-GAAP Measures." CFO.com (27 September): ww2.cfo.com/accounting/2016/09/minding-non-gaap-measures.

Bhattacharya, N., E. Black, T. Christensen, and C. Larson. 2003. "Assessing the Relative Informativeness and Permanence of Pro Forma Earnings and GAAP Operating Earnings." *Journal of Accounting and Economics*, vol. 36, no. 1: 285–319.

Black, D., and T. Christensen. 2009. "US Managers' Use of 'Pro Forma' Adjustments to Meet Strategic Earnings Targets." *Journal of Business Finance & Accounting*, vol. 36, no. 3–4 (April/May): 297–326.

Brown, S., K. Lo, and T. Lys. 1999. "Use of R^2 in Accounting Research: Measuring Changes in Value Relevance over the Last Four Decades." *Journal of Accounting and Economics*, vol. 28, no. 2 (December): 83–115.

Brown, L.D., A.C. Call, M.B. Clement, and N.Y. Sharp. 2015. "Inside the 'Black Box' of Sell-Side Financial Analysts." *Journal of Accounting Research*, vol. 53, no. 1 (March): 1–47.

Center for Audit Quality. 2016. "Questions on Non-GAAP Measures: A Tool for Audit Committees" (www.thecaq.org/sites/default/files/questions_on_non-gaap_measures_final.pdf).

CFA Institute. 2007. *A Comprehensive Business Reporting Model: Financial Reporting for Investors* (7 July): www.cfainstitute.org/learning/products/publications/ccb/Pages/ccb.v2007.n6.4818.aspx.

CFA Society United Kingdom. 2015. "Non-IFRS Earnings and Alternative Performance Measures: Ensuring a Level Playing Field" (July): https://secure.cfauk.org/assets/1345/Non_IFRS_Earnings_and_Alternative_Performance_Measures___FINAL_web.pdf.

Chang, James. 1999. "The Decline in Value Relevance of Earnings and Book Values." Working paper, University of Pennsylvania.

Chapman, M., and M. Vaessen. 2016. "Room for Improvement: The KPMG Survey of Business Reporting," 2nd ed. (28 April): https://home.kpmg.com/xx/en/home/insights/2016/04/kpmg-survey-business-reporting-second-edition.html.

Ciesielski, J. 2016. "Wonder Bread: Non-GAAP Earnings Keep Rising in the S&P 500." *Analyst's Accounting Observer*, vol. 25, no. 4 (March).

Collins, D.W., E.L. Maydew, and I.S. Weiss. 1997. "Changes in the Value-Relevance of Earnings and Book Values over the Past Forty Years." *Journal of Accounting and Economics*, vol. 24, no. 1 (December): 39–67.

Dechow, P.M., and C. Schrand. 2004. *Earnings Quality*. Charlottesville, VA: CFA Institute Research Foundation.

Deloitte. 2015. "SEC Comment Letters, Including Industry Insights: What "Edgar" Told Us" (October).

———. 2016. "Alternative Performance Measures: IFRS in Focus: A Practical Guide" (27 July): www2.deloitte.com/content/dam/Deloitte/ru/Documents/audit/IFRS_news/july-27-2016.pdf.

Dichev, D.I., J. Graham, C.R. Harvey, and S. Rajgopal. 2015. "The Misrepresentation of Earnings." Working paper, Goizueta Business School, National Bureau of Economic Research, and Columbia Business School.

ESMA. 2015. "ESMA Guidelines on Alternative Performance Measures" (October): www.esma.europa.eu/sites/default/files/library/2015/10/2015-esma-1415en.pdf.

Financial Reporting Council. 2014. *FRC ARP Staff Research Report: Investor Views on Intangible Assets and Their Amortisation* (March): https://frc.org.uk/Our-Work/Publications/Accounting-and-Reporting-Policy/Research-Report-Investor-Views-on-Intangible-Asset.pdf.

Francis, J., and K. Schipper. 1999. "Have Financial Statements Lost Their Relevance?" *Journal of Accounting Research*, vol. 37, no. 2 (Autumn): 319–352.

Frankel, R., S. McVay, and M. Soliman. 2011. "Non-GAAP Earnings and Board Independence." *Review of Accounting Studies*, vol. 16, no. 4 (December): 719–744.

Holland, S.C., P. Kernan, R. Verdes, and J.T. Joseph. 2014. "Why Inconsistent Reporting of Exceptional Items Can Cloud Underlying Profitability at Nonfinancial FTSE 100 Companies." Standard and Poor's Ratings Services, *Credit Week* (26 February).

Hoogervorst, H. 2015. "Non-GAAP Numbers May Confuse Investors: SEC Chair." *CFO Journal* (9 December): http://www.ifrs.org/Alerts/Conference/Documents/2015/Speech-Hans-Mind-the-Gap-speech-Korea-March-2015.pdf.

Institute of Chartered Accountants of Scotland. 2016. "What Is Performance? An ICAS Discussion Paper and Call for Research" (www.icas.com/__data/assets/pdf_file/0004/243967/ICAS-What-is-performance.pdf).

IOSCO. 2016. "Statement on Non-GAAP Financial Measures. Final Report" (June): www.iosco.org/library/pubdocs/pdf/IOSCOPD532.pdf.

Isidiro, H., and A. Marques. 2009. "Beating Strategic Earnings Benchmarks with Non-GAAP Figures: International Evidence." Working paper (1 September): http://papers.ssrn.com/sol3/papers.cfm?abstract_id=1465677.

Joshi, S.J., J.T. Joseph, and V. Velandy. 2014. "Non-GAAP Measures Are Useful, but Could Benefit from Standard Definitions and Independent Assurances." Standard and Poor's Ratings Services, *Credit Week* (26 February).

Kaplan, M.E., J.M. Samit, L.M. Isaacson, and D.M. Becker. 2016. "Early Returns: Companies Change Non-GAAP Financial Disclosures Following Recently Issued SEC Guidance." *CLS Blue Sky Blog* (8 September): http://clsbluesky.law.columbia.edu/2016/09/08/early-returns-companies-change-non-gaap-financial-disclosures-following-recently-issued-sec-guidance.

Kolev, K., C.A. Marquardt, and S.E. McVay. 2008. "SEC Scrutiny and the Evolution of Non-GAAP Reporting." *Accounting Review*, vol. 81, no. 1: 157–184.

Lev, B., and F. Gu. 2016. *The End of Accounting and the Path Forward for Investors and Managers*. Hoboken, NJ: John Wiley & Sons.

Lev, B., and P. Zarowin. 1999. "The Boundaries of Financial Reporting and How to Extend Them." *Journal of Accounting Research*, vol. 37, no. 2 (Autumn): 353–385.

Linsmeier, T. 2016. "Tom Linsmeier Looks to the Future as He Leaves the Board." Financial Accounting Standards Board (Q2): www.fasb.org/jsp/FASB/Page/SectionPage&cid=1176168083404.

Marcogliese, Pam, and Dase Kim. 2016. "Non-GAAP: The Pendulum Swings Back." *Corporate Governance Advisor*, vol. 24, no. 4 (July/August): http://paygovernance.com/wp-content/uploads/2016/06/7-16.pdf.

Melumad, N.D., and D. Nissim. 2008. "Foundation and Trends in Accounting." *Now: The Essence of Knowledge*, vol. 3, no. 2–3: 87–221.

Papa, V.T., and S.J. Peters. 2013. *User Perspectives on Financial Instrument Risk Disclosures under International Financial Reporting Standards: Derivatives and Hedging Activities Disclosures (Volume 2)*. CFA Institute (January): www.cfainstitute.org/ethics/Documents/cfa_institute_user_perspectives_on_financial_instruments_under_ifrs.pdf.

———. 2015. *Analyzing Bank Performance: Role of Comprehensive Income*. CFA Institute (February): www.cfainstitute.org/learning/products/publications/ccb/Pages/ccb.v2015.n3.1.aspx.

———. 2016. *Investor Uses, Expectations, and Concerns on Non-GAAP Financial Measures*. CFA Institute (October).

Parker, Adam S. 2016. “North America Insight: The GAAP Gap—Does it Matter?” Morgan Stanley US Equity Strategy (20 April).

Penman, S.H., and X.-J. Zhang. 2002. “Accounting Conservatism, the Quality of Earnings, and Stock Returns.” *Accounting Review*, vol. 77, no. 2 (April): 237–264.

PwC. 2014. “Corporate Performance: What Do Investors Want to Know? Reporting Adjusted Performance Measures” (July): www.pwc.com/gx/en/audit-services/corporate-reporting/assets/pdfs/pwc-reporting-adjusted-performance-measures.pdf

———. 2016. “Building Confidence in Non-GAAP Measures and Other KPIs” (www.pwc.com/us/en/cfodirect/assets/pdf/non-gaap-measures-other-kpis.pdf).

Shamrock, E.S. 2012. *IFRS and US GAAP: A Comprehensive Comparison*. Edison, NJ: John Wiley & Sons.

Sherman, D.H., and D.S. Young. 2016. “Where Financial Reporting Still Falls Short.” *Harvard Business Review* (July–August): https://hbr.org/2016/07/where-financial-reporting-still-falls-short.

Siegel, M. 2016. “For the Investor: The Use of Non-GAAP Metrics.” FASB (www.fasb.org/jsp/FASB/Page/SectionPage&cid=1176164442130).

Young, S. 2013. “The Drivers, Consequences and Policy Implications of Non-GAAP Reporting.” ICAEW Better Markets Conference (November).

8. Appendix: Member Survey Respondent Profile

Figure 8.1. Respondents by Functional Role

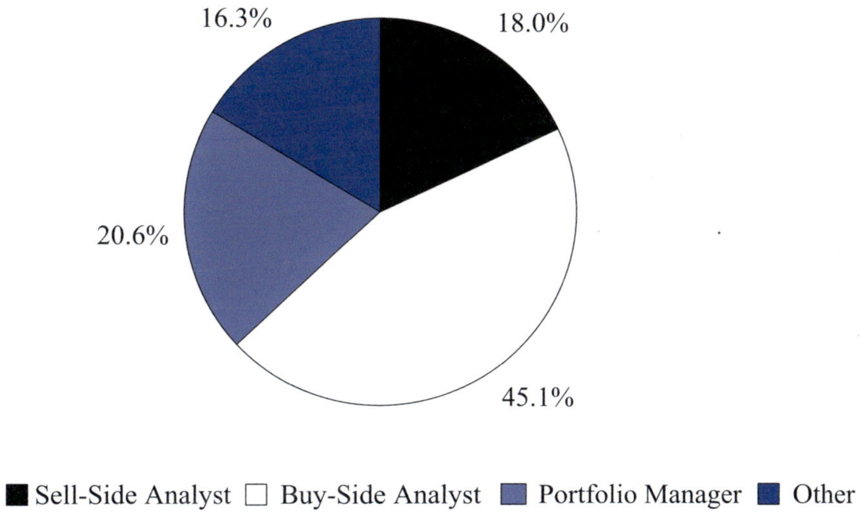

Figure 8.2. Respondents by Asset Class

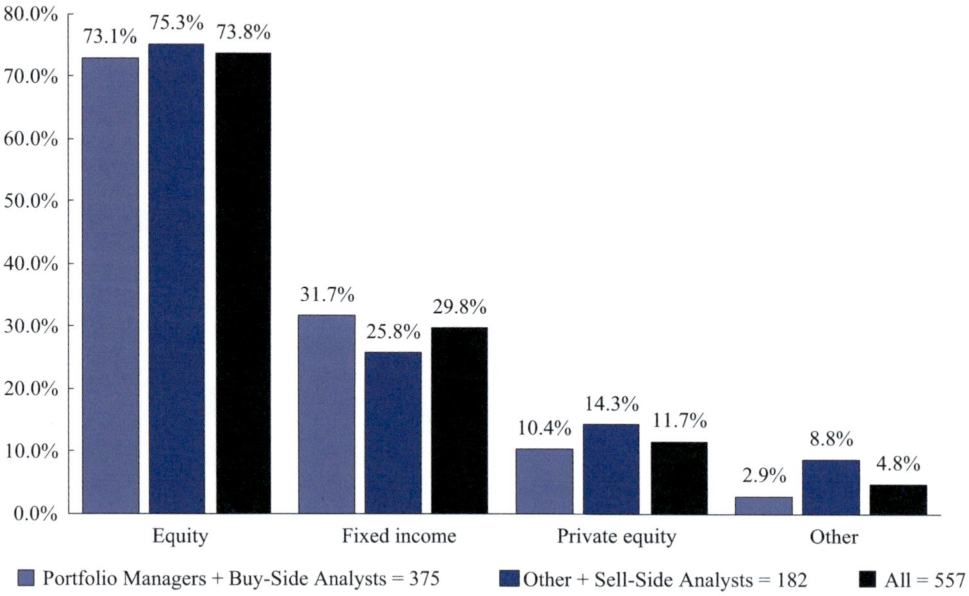

Figure 8.3. Respondents by Investment Horizon

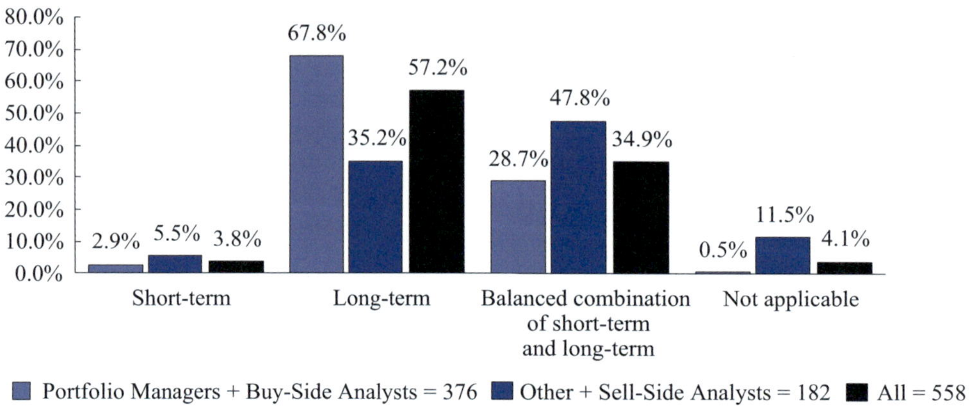

Figure 8.4A. Sectors Covered by Respondents

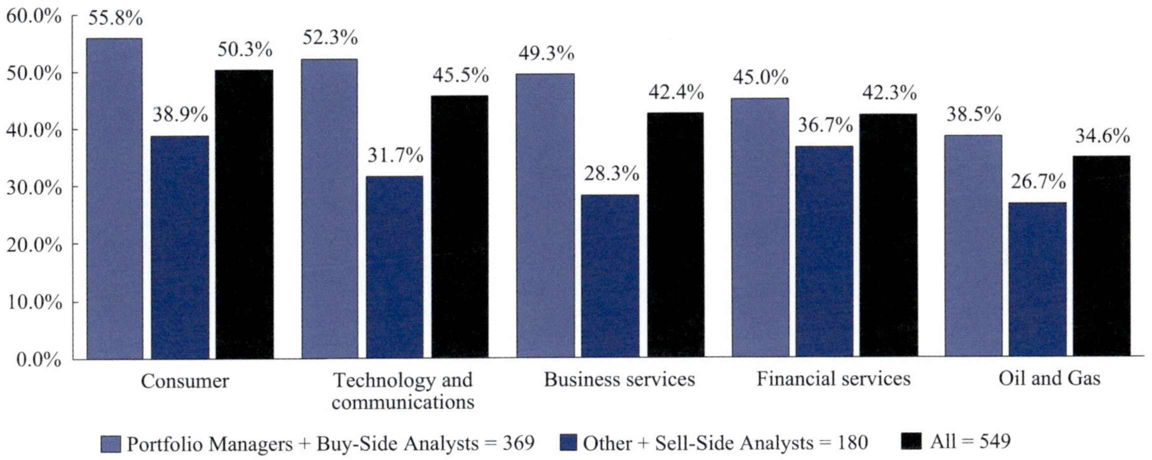

Figure 8.4B. Sectors Covered by Respondents (continued)

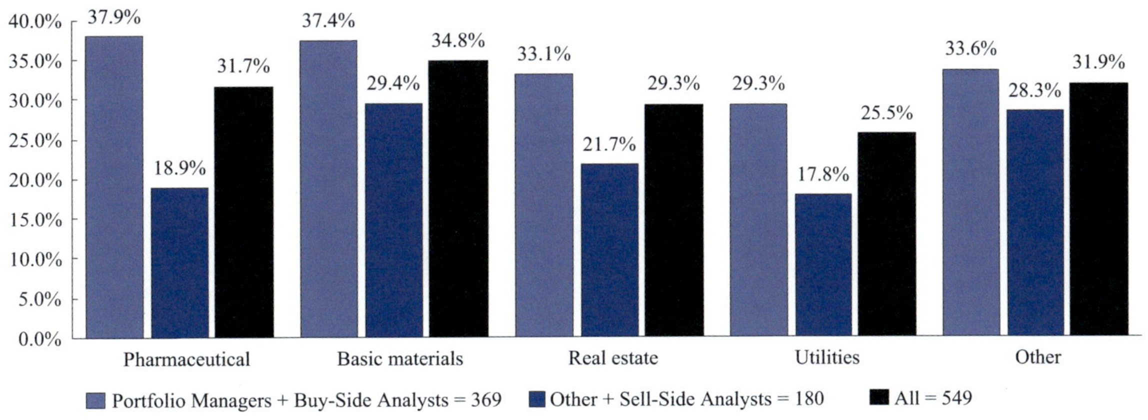

CFA Institute

AUTHORS

Vincent T. Papa, PhD, CPA, CFA
Interim Head
Financial Reporting Policy

Sandra J. Peters, CPA, CFA
Head
Financial Reporting Policy

CONTRIBUTOR

Kurt Schacht, JD, CFA
Managing Director
Standards and Advocacy

We are thankful for helpful comments from various reviewers, including Hilary Eastman, CFA, of PricewaterhouseCoopers; Marietta Miemietz, CFA, of Primavenue Advisory Services; Erin Greenfield, CFA, of Trimark Investments; Richard Schreuder, CFA, of Saemor Capital; Tony Sondhi of A.C. Sondhi and Associates; Gerry White, CFA, of Grace and White Associates; and the following IFRS Foundation staff members: Fred Nieto, CFA; Rachel Knubley; Michelle Fisher; Suzanne Morsfield; Eduardo Damasio of ESMA. We're also thankful for input from Jason Voss, CFA, content director, CFA Institute.

We also thank Jack Ciesielski, CFA, of R.G. Associates and Mark O'Sullivan of PricewaterhouseCoopers for participating as key speakers in a related CFA Institute member webcast in June 2016. Their perspectives and published work helped inform our understanding of key issues around the reporting of non-GAAP financial measures.